This Book Belongs To
The Ethical Culture Society of
Silicon Valley

ETHICS AS A RELIGION

David Saville Muzzey

"WHAT DOTH THE LORD REQUIRE
OF THEE, BUT TO DO JUSTLY, AND
TO LOVE MERCY, AND TO WALK
HUMBLY WITH THY GOD?"
Micah 6:8

Introduction by *James F. Hornback*

An American Ethical Union Publication

"Ethics As a Religion," by David Saville Muzzey. ISBN 978-0-9897323-7-6.

Published by The American Ethical Union ©2013. All rights reserved. No part of this publication may be reproduced, stored in a retrieval system, or transmitted in any form or by any means, electronic, mechanical, recording or otherwise, without the prior written permission of The American Ethical Union.

Manufactured in the United States of America.

Introduction

FOR DAVID S. MUZZEY there was never any doubt about the religious character of the Ethical Culture movement. "If it were not religious, I would never have joined it," he liked to say, with all the assurance of Dr. Johnson kicking a stone to prove the reality of matter. Yet he knew loyal members of the movement who preferred not to call it religious, and millions of the more traditionally religious who were reluctant to describe as "religious" a group, however ethical, which declined to take a positive stand on questions of theology.

When the time came for him to set down a "spiritual autobiography" in 1951, "beginning my ninth decade," Dr. Muzzey collected his most recent and pertinent addresses and called the collection simply "Ethical Religion." Four of the addresses had appeared earlier in a pamphlet with the same title, and even the galley proofs of the enlarged version came back from the printer as *Ethical Religion*. As a junior colleague, under his guidance then as leader of the Westchester Ethical Society, I called his attention to the possibility of getting more of a message into the title. Many potential

INTRODUCTION

readers, not to say reviewers, tend to stop short at the title of a book if they are not given a more explicit clue to the contents.

Dr. Muzzey yielded readily to the suggestion, granting that there are indeed several widely recognized ethical religions—world faiths such as Buddhism, Judaism, Confucianism, and Christianity, in which the ethical factor is prominent if not predominant. There are indeed several books entitled *Ethical Religion,* including one published in 1889 by William Mackintire Salter of Chicago, whom many regard as the leading philosopher of the first generation of Ethical leaders. But there is only one fellowship, so far as we know, which is devoted exclusively to the propagation of universal, humanitarian ethics as a religion. Dr. Muzzey believed in such fellowship, whatever its actual designation, as essential to the development and practice of an ethical faith. The title finally selected for his book, *Ethics as a Religion,* gives the key to his main line of thought.

Students of the world's religions have long compared them in their three most obvious aspects, those of creed, cult, and code. Similarly in Chapter 9, "A Religion for Adults," Dr. Muzzey points to "the doctrinal, the ceremonial, and the ethical" facets of religious life and teaching. He would have us reverse the order of importance attached to these facets in Western religions, and in Christianity in particular, by placing the greatest emphasis upon the ethical component, leaving the ceremonial purely as a matter of individual taste and tem-

INTRODUCTION

perament, and relegating the doctrinal element to "its place among the historical survivals of man's early conceptions of science, philosophy, and social duties."

Among the reviewers of the first edition of *Ethics as a Religion,* published in 1951, there was frank skepticism about this downgrading of the ceremonial and doctrinal components of religion. The grounds for this skepticism were not fundamentalist or orthodox, for the most part, but psychological and scientific. May not the creed and the cult loom larger in a functional and natural religion, as indeed they seemed to do in Dr. Muzzey's own life? And should they not do so, as a matter of responsible ethics?

There was in Dr. Muzzey that old-fashioned, absolute integrity from which sprang his tendency to accept the solemn expressions of faith and motive of others at face value. To the charge of some reviewers that he was really an "unconscious Christian," for all his protestations of emancipation and disbelief, he answered stoutly that he was a "conscious non-Christian," thus digging himself in deeper with the depth psychologists.

To friendly as well as to unfriendly critics, he did not seem to respond fully to the charge that his own ethical "postulates" had some of the dogmatic, traditional, and supernatural character he criticized in the doctrines of the churches and temples. Some of us like to make our sanctions more explicit. Yet it seemed evident to Dr. Muzzey, without the sanction of scientific naturalism or of any of the more empirical philosophies of experience, that there is "a moral law in the universe, as permeating and indefeasible as the physical laws of nature," and "a spiritual element in man's nature which makes him capable of seeking the fulfillment of the moral law in his daily conduct." Man has the consequent "responsibility to demonstrate that capacity in his relations with his fellow men."

It was precisely the seriousness and integrity of his boyhood faith which led him to abandon that faith. Many of us have heard his story, as recorded in Chapter 2, of the hypocritical host, or one with a double standard for laymen and clergy, who tried to hide the Sunday paper from him when he was a student at Union Seminary and preaching at a suburban New York church. Then there is the story, recounted in Chapter 13, of the breaking of his own "religious provincialism" when as a young teacher at Robert College, Constantinople (now Istanbul), he stood as "a despised infidel" on the balcony of the Mosque of Santa Sophia while thousands of pious Moslems celebrated the last night of the Holy Month of Ramadan.

It was this stubborn Yankee integrity and fidelity to fact which made David Muzzey a controversial historian and teacher. His basic textbook, *An American History,* was first published in 1911 and then revised and reprinted every two to six years, with occasional variation in title, for forty years. He scandalized patriotic Americans with his objectivity, internationalism, and debunking of myths. In 1922, for example, a citizens' associa-

INTRODUCTION

tion in the District of Columbia complained that Dr. Muzzey's book had given only a single line to John Paul Jones, and that the author had charged Congress with graft and corruption.

"History wasn't history in those days," he recalled in a newspaper interview more than twenty years later. "It was just a soft public relations job. I used to get ten letters a day challenging me to duels for not being respectful enough to George Washington, Robert E. Lee, the Supreme Court and the original colony of Georgia, which I pointed out had been started by James Oglethorpe as a haven for convicts."

Dr. Muzzey's own two ancestors killed in the American Revolution, and his birth and boyhood in Lexington, Massachusetts, made little impression on such critics as the Sons of the American Revolution, Mayor "Big Bill" Thompson of Chicago, William Randolph Hearst, and the Board of Education of Savannah, Georgia. Nor did his record of graduation with highest honors from Harvard in 1893, from Union Theological Seminary in 1897, and from Columbia University with a Ph.D. in 1907 after studies in history and classics in Paris and Berlin. His early reputation as an American historian was so colored by pacifism and internationalism that few critics seemed to notice his religious heresies.

He had joined the Society for Ethical Culture in 1898, as a promising assistant to Felix Adler in the Society's adult education program. In 1899 he began to

INTRODUCTION

teach Latin and history in the Ethical Culture School, and in 1905 Dr. Adler chose him as an associate leader of the society. Dr. Muzzey retained a part-time professional relationship with the New York Society throughout his long teaching career at Barnard College and Columbia University, which included such special assignments as the Carnegie Lectures in American History in Paris, Prague, and Edinburgh, and ended with his retirement as Governor Morris Professor of History at Columbia in 1940. He also served as advisory leader to the Westchester Ethical Society from its beginnings in 1921 until his request for emeritus status there and in New York in 1950.

His pacifism became a public scandal early in 1917, while he was teaching at Barnard College. In a Lincoln's Birthday address he said, in defense of peace rather than German policies, "Before going to war I would wait until they had sunk seven ships. Yes, I would wait until they had sunk seventy times seven ships and then I wouldn't go to war." Dr. Nicholas Murray Butler, President of Columbia University, resisted the clamor for his dismissal with a firm affirmation of academic and personal freedom. Soon, however, Dr. Muzzey himself decided that the Germans had gone too far, piling "outrage upon outrage," and supported American participation in the war.

In the 1920's critics of his internationalism seized upon his pro-British attitudes and his English interpretations of American history. Mayor Thompson banned

INTRODUCTION

Muzzey textbooks from the public schools of Chicago, and illustrated speeches in defense of the ban by pointing to a cage holding a live rat which was scurrilously labeled "Muzzey." Hearst papers all over the nation ran cartoons of a rat of the same name, gnawing at the foundations of an American schoolhouse.

For the most part, Dr. Muzzey allowed historical facts to speak for themselves, and saved philosophizing for his books and addresses within the Ethical movement. In our age of freer criticism, his history textbooks seem long on facts and short on interpretation, thought they do contain paragraphs like the following —from the preface to his college text, *The United States of America*:

> Our destiny is not the making of money, but the making of America. Our heritage of political ideals is a far richer possession than our heritage of natural resources: for if the ideals be lost or obscured, all the treasures of field, factory and mine cannot avail to save us from the fate of Ninevah or Rome.

These lines may seem as "un-American" to some of our contemporaries as they did to many of Dr. Muzzey's.

Despite his public identification with history and politics, through his textbooks and his biographies of Jefferson and James G. Blaine, Dr. Muzzey maintained a wide range of interests which he used as subject matter for his writings. His published works include an early Latin grammar, a study of Church and State in relation to the schools of France, *The Rise of the New*

INTRODUCTION

Testament, The Spiritual Franciscans, and the recently reissued *Spiritual Heroes,* a study of Jeremiah, Buddha, Socrates, Jesus, St. Paul, Marcus Aurelius, St. Augustine, Mohammed, and Martin Luther.

In the first half of his "ninth decade" anticipated in the present book, Dr. Muzzey remained remarkably active. Reluctantly, on medical advice, he gave up swimming, tennis, and softball in favor of a straight game of golf and such spectator sports as watching his favorite New York Yankees on television. Latterly, he and his wife, Emilie, a former teaching colleague at Barnard, divided their time between his old home in Yonkers, where he lived for more than fifty years, and their summer place in Annisquam, Massachusetts.

As a Leader Emeritus in both the New York and Westchester Societies, he continued as a speaker and adviser throughout the American Ethical Union. (He had been chairman of the Fraternity of Leaders in his senior active years, and an early editor of the American Ethical Union journal, *The Standard.*) His tours took him and his wife throughout the Atlantic states and as far away as the St. Louis Society, where he celebrated his eighty-second birthday in October, 1952, maintaining his reputation as an after-dinner speaker and raconteur. He also spoke on the following Sunday morning at Sheldon Memorial Meeting House, as he had every year or two since the dedication there in October, 1912. His characteristically pertinent topic was "Forty Years in the Wilderness."

INTRODUCTION

In his prime, Dr. Muzzey always spoke extemporaneously, relying on wide scholarship, quick wit, and a prodigious memory. But the essays in the present book were prepared first for oral reading as Sunday addresses, and later edited for continuity. They reflect a life faith which "grows stronger," as he put it in his foreword to the first edition—a "faith in the reasonableness, the timeliness, the adequacy, and the eventual triumph of the Religion of Ethics."

In the last few years of his long life, with the ebbing of his strength and the failure and then partial renewal of his eyesight, Mrs. Muzzey kept him in touch with world affairs and with the timeless world of literature and history, which he remembered best, but he grew increasingly out of touch with those of us who had known him as a friend, teacher, adviser, and fellow worker. He died on April 14, 1965, six months short of his ninety-fifth birthday.

We are happy and proud, in this third year after his death, to introduce a new printing and wider circulation of "the spiritual autobiography of a seeker for the soul's peace."

JAMES F. HORNBACK
Ethical Society of St. Louis

Foreword

THAT THERE IS *today a revival of interest in religion is shown by the number of books, pamphlets and magazine articles published on the subject. Nor is the cause far to seek. Forty years mankind has been wandering in the wilderness; and no rod has smitten the rock to send forth the water to quench man's thirst for peace, no manna has fallen from heaven to assuage his spiritual hunger. The Promised Land, so clear to the vision of a Woodrow Wilson, is but "dimly seen" through the mists of mutual defiance and haunting fear. The generation that has come to middle age with the century has lived through a succession of crises, political, economic and social, which have shaken its faith in the competence of man to achieve his goal of a free and ordered world.*

Religion, like every other subject of human interest, is affected by the current unsettled "climate of opinion." Its spokesmen cry Lo! here and Lo! there. On one point, however, there is agreement among Catholics, Protestants and Jews; believers, skeptics and agnostics. That is that religion today is undergoing a transformation of major importance. It is no longer a question of the preference of one sect over another, as it was in our fathers' day. The very bases on which all the religious creeds and ceremonies were founded—a providential God, a divine revelation, an authoritative scripture or priesthood, an endless future of rewards and punishment—are all called in question. No one can tell to what extent "honest doubt" has invaded the pulpit and the pews, or how far conviction has yielded to conformity.

If by the rationalists this parlous state of organized religion is welcomed as a promise of the end of superstition, the vast majority, agreeing with Gilbert Chesterton that a man's religion is the most important thing in his life, hope for a renewal rather than a repudiation of religious faith. This need is constantly stressed, not only by the professional leaders, but by public officials from the President down and by businessmen, educators and social workers, who urge that a religious faith is necessary to combat the materialism and the moral hebetude of the present age. The all-important question is, What kind of religion will be adequate to meet the needs of modern man? And this book is offered as an attempt to answer that question. There is no striving for philosophical profundity or theological subtlety in these pages. They are written in simple, straightforward language as an invitation to honest, fearless and independent thinking on the vital subject of religion. They are an invitation to the reader to compare his religious experience with mine and to weigh with an unprejudiced mind what he considers to be the merits or the faults of my argument.

FOREWORD

Though any attempt at a fresh inquiry into religion must necessarily controvert some accepted doctrines and practices, my purpose is not so much to attack what seems to me error as to affirm what seems to me truth. "A man's faith," as Carlyle said, "does not consist in what he does not believe." Demolition is warranted only as it is necessary for new construction. Not all the old is error and not all the new is truth; but the truth in the old must always be verified by new insights, new knowledge, new courage. Time plays havoc with static conceptions.

Above all let me insist that there is naught set down in malice or disdain in these pages. Sincere devotion to any form of religion commands my respect for the devotee, however sharp my dissent from his doctrines may be. I prize the friendship of many devout Roman Catholics, Protestants and Jews, and I am sure that these friends do not allow their disapproval of my religious views to disturb their friendship for me. After all, we are all together embarked on the quest for truth. We are all passengers on the ship that is seeking port through the storms and fogs of this earthly life. And in this perilous voyage we all need what any one of us can contribute of mental enlightenment, moral courage and spiritual vision.

This, then, is my testament: the spiritual autobiography of a seeker for the soul's peace. The shadows lengthen. I am beginning my ninth decade of life. But as the years recede my faith grows stronger; faith in the reasonableness, the timeliness, the adequacy, and the eventual triumph of the Religion of Ethics.

Table of Contents

1. *Introductory* — 1
2. *Priestly and Prophetic Religion* — 6
3. *The Seat of Authority in Religion* — 19
4. *Ethical Religion and Christianity* — 32
5. *Intellectual Piety* — 50
6. *The Elements of Ethical Religion* — 70
7. *An Ethical Concept of God* — 86
8. *Is Ethics Enough?* — 100
9. *A Religion for Adults* — 119
10. *Ethical Fellowship* — 135
11. *The Postulates of Ethical Religion* — 152

12.	*Our Ethical Heritage*	**168**
13.	*Religious Provincialism*	**188**
14.	*The Timeliness of Ethical Religion*	**207**
15.	*Enduring Values in Religion*	**226**
16.	*The Future of Ethical Religion*	**241**

EPILOGUE

The Founding of the Ethical Movement   **258**

ETHICS AS A RELIGION

CHAPTER ONE

INTRODUCTORY

T his book is frankly a piece of propaganda. Its purpose is to recommend to the reader a type of religion differing in important respects from the doctrines on which the faith of the churches and the synagogues is built. Not that Ethical Culture is a novelty. All through the centuries of Christendom there have been advocates

ETHICS AS A RELIGION

of a religious reform which should shift the emphasis from dogma to ethics, from creed to deed, from supernatural revelation to human responsibility, from a theocentric to an anthropocentric philosophy of life. In line with this tradition, and seeking to fortify it, is the Ethical Culture movement. And because it puts forth the claim to be a religion, it is incumbent on its adherents to explain to those who contest this claim the principles on which the claim rests. The question is constantly asked of the leaders and members of the movement, What does Ethical Culture stand for? Therefore we give here a brief statement of the basic principles of the movement, which will be developed in more detail in the chapters which follow.

First, Ethical Culture is a creedless religion. The bond of union among its members is a common devotion to the cultivation of moral excellence as the chief duty of man. Contrary to the widely accepted teaching that right conduct depends as a corollary on correct religious belief, we hold that it is the conscientious striving for righteousness in thought and action that has constantly refined and humanized the dogmas of the creeds: in a word, that it is not the church that makes good men, but good men who make the church.

Second, Ethical Culture insists that man has the capacity as well as the duty to lead a righteous life. Its postulate of the infinite and induplicable worth of every human being necessarily involves the belief that it is within the power of every human being to choose at every step be-

INTRODUCTORY

tween a right and a wrong course of action. It utterly rejects the will-paralyzing doctrine of the corruption of man through Adam's fall. That man sins against his fellow men is evident enough; but that he is compelled to do so by his very nature is an insult to his dignity. If he has in him proclivities to evil, it is no less true that he has promptings to good. All that we know of good and evil is furnished by human actions. Ethical religion distinguishes sharply between a man's *value* to society (which may be nil) and his *worth* as an individual with latent capacities for moral improvement.

Third, since the attainment of ethical stature is the chief end of life, the development of these latent capacities in one's self and in others is the serious task of the adherents of ethical religion. And the method which it prescribes for the accomplishment of this task differs from the two rules of conduct most generally recommended: namely, the categorical imperative of Kant and the Golden Rule of the Gospel. The former bids us so to act that our conduct could be taken as the universal norm; the latter bids us to do to others as we would have them do to us. But neither counsel is quite satisfying. For no sane man would presume to set up his own conduct as a pattern to be followed. Nor should our treatment of others be based on what might be expected from them under different circumstances. This is unrealistic and even suggests something in the nature of a bargain. The rule: So act in all your relationships, in the family, in business, in politics in the professions, as to elicit the best in others, and in so doing you will enhance your own worth. This is the very sum and substance of the ethical imperative.

Fourth, ethical religion neither affirms nor denies the truth of certain propositions which are generally accepted by the churches, such as the existence of God, the immortality of the soul, and rewards and punishments in a future life. It respects the convictions of the individual, but seeks no conformity of belief in philosophical or theological matters. It recognizes that such beliefs may be instrumental to the supreme end of the cultivation of ethical character; but it distinguishes between belief in propositions which transcend human reason and propositions which offend human reason. It insists upon intellectual integrity as the hallmark of man's dignity, and totally rejects such insults to human reason as Tertullian's *"Credo quia absurdum."*

Fifth and finally, ethical religion offers a platform on which men of good will of every clime and race can unite. In the agonized world of today the peoples of every freedom-loving nation are seeking through united effort to put an end to the rule of strife and slaughter. But all the work of statesmen and diplomats will avail nothing unless it is inspired by a "common faith" in the power of man to shape his destiny. This power comes from religion. But the religious world is sorely divided. In our own country more than two hundred creeds and sects exist in rivalry. The great religious systems of the East can no longer be dismissed in Calvin's scornful phrase as "a vast welter of

INTRODUCTORY

error." Nor will they yield to Christianity. But Buddhist, Taoist, Mohammedan, Parsi, and Hindu could all unite on the broad basis of ethical religion. For its appeal is to aspirations and obligations which are native to the heart of man.

CHAPTER TWO

PRIESTLY AND PROPHETIC RELIGION

Through the ages religion has taken on a vast and varied number of forms. But in all this variety two types of religion are clearly distinguishable: the priestly and the prophetic. Of these the priestly type is by far the older and more prevalent.

PRIESTLY AND PROPHETIC RELIGION

Primitive peoples, ignorant of the forces of nature and filled with wonder and fear in the face of the mysteries of storm and flood, of birth and sickness and death, sought explanation in the existence of unseen powers that controlled man's destiny. To win the favor of these powers or avert their wrath men devised many elaborate ceremonies, such as are described in Sir James G. Frazer's classic volumes entitled *The Golden Bough*. Naturally, the man who came forward to preside at the ceremonies and interpret the will of the unseen powers gained a position of supreme influence over the tribe. He guarded this influence jealously, claiming exclusive access to the spirit powers and devising secret charms and spells to awe the people. It was priesthood in its lowest form: wizardry, shamanism, magic "medicine."

When the great monarchies arose in the East, the kings enhanced their prowess as conquerors by alliance with the priests. Indeed, the king himself often assumed priestly functions and claimed descent from the gods. Hence the origin of the doctrine of the "divine right" of kings which prevailed through the Middle Ages and some traces of which have lasted to our own days. In *Hamlet* Claudius relies upon "the divinity that doth hedge a king" to protect him from the wrath of Laertes. People with scurvy approached the dissolute King Charles II as he walked with his courtiers from Whitehall to St. James's, that they might be cured by the "king's touch." The king archon in ancient Greece was a priest. And the first office to which Julius Caesar was elected was that of Pontifex Maximus, or chief priest of Rome, a sort of pagan pope.

ETHICS AS A RELIGION

The early Christian church had no priesthood. It was a body of believers in the proximate return of Christ to inaugurate the kingdom of God on earth as a preparation for the eternal kingdom of heaven. It was the enemy of the political state, enduring cruel persecutions for its refusal to acknowledge the divine authority of Caesar. But in the fourth century the Emperor Constantine adopted Christianity as the state religion and became a lavish patron of the church. He still tolerated the pagan rites; but a few years later the Emperor Theodosius published his famous code which made the worship of the old gods of Rome a political crime. So was cemented that baleful union of state and church, of throne and altar, of politics and religion, which for centuries has plagued the world. Not that the throne and the altar were always in harmony in their alliance. During the Middle Ages the temporal and spiritual powers fought bitter battles for supremacy, battles whose echoes have come down in the strife between church and state in many European countries. Witness the Waldeck-Rousseau and Combes ministries in France, the May Laws of Bismarck's Germany, and Mussolini's cynical violations of the pact of 1929 with the Vatican. And in our own land, in spite of the constitutional provision for the separation of church and state, one branch of the Christian church does not cease to ask for a part of the public funds for the support of its parochial schools. The great Italian poet Dante deplored the "fatal gift" of Constantine, when that emperor bestowed upon the church the lands which started it on its path of temporal political power.

Priestly religion in the countries of Christendom is most completely represented by the Roman Catholic Church. Its hierarchy culminates in the pope, who, by the Vatican decree of 1870, is infallible when he pronounces on questions of faith or morals. There is no appeal. His decree is final, like a decision of our Supreme Court. To be sure, there is a democratic element in the church, in that a person of any social class may become a priest and rise to the highest place in the hierarchy, even to the papacy. The great medieval Pope Hildebrand (Gregory VII) was the son of a carpenter, and Pius X (Sarto) was a peasant priest of northern Italy. But once consecrated, the priest becomes a member of a strictly authoritative institution. He is bound by irrevocable vows. The limits of his thinking are set by the dogmas of the church. Even if his intellect be as keen as that of a Thomas Aquinas, he must not use it to conclusions contradicting the faith delivered to the fathers. His mind is free—within limits prescribed by the church. But a limited mental freedom suggests a contradiction in terms.

Again, priestly religion is static in a dynamic age. It looks back to doctrines and ceremonies assumed to be unchanging and unchangeable. The spirit of free inquiry, to which mankind owes every advance in science, politics, education and social reform, is foreign to its nature. As Andrew D. White showed in his volumes on *The Warfare*

ETHICS AS A RELIGION

Between Science and Theology, the church, both Catholic and Protestant, resisted at its source every discovery in science that threatened to make obsolete its theories of astronomy, geology, biology, chronology, etc., based on alleged divine revelation. And when the acceptance of the new truth became inevitable, its recognition by the church was grudging and belated.

A third characteristic of priestly religion is the sharp line it draws between the clergy (*kleros,* or set apart) and the laity. In the Catholic Church the clergy inspire awe in the laity, because of their privilege of administering the sacraments of the mass, baptism, confirmation, confession and extreme unction, which control the religious life of the parishioner from the cradle to the grave. The priest is the channel through which divine grace flows. His consecration is indelible. In the Protestant sects the line between the minister and his congregation is not so sharply drawn; and yet there is a kind of restraint or embarrassment often felt in the presence of a clergyman. Emerson once said that when a minister entered a room conversation ceased. Many years ago a little incident occurred to show me what Emerson meant. As a senior in the theological seminary I was supplying the pulpit of a small church in the suburbs of New York. When I came down the stairs to enter the living room on Sunday morning, I caught a glimpse of my host for the week-end hurriedly throwing the Sunday newspaper behind a screen. This gesture, though it was doubtless meant as a mark of respect for the "cloth," disgusted me so that I was never ordained as a minister. If I could not be treated as a normal man instead of as a pious symbol, the ministry had no appeal for me. I would take no vows that set me apart from my fellow men and implied the bestowal of a special spiritual character.

Besides manifesting these elements of autocracy, ultraconservatism and clerical restraint, priestly religion is chargeable with subordinating morality (which Matthew Arnold declared to be four-fifths of life) to orthodox belief and prescribed ritual. This is by no means to imply that priestly religion is indifferent to morality, but only that it regards moral conduct as a corollary to correct belief. Fidelity to the creed is the primary requirement, and heresy, or departure from the true faith, has always been treated more severely by the church than moral lapses. No man was ever burned at the stake for adultery; but thousands have been tortured and killed for denying the Trinity or refusing obedience to the dictates of the hierarchy. The most cruel wars in history (at least up to the twentieth century) have been fought over religious doctrines; and when they were over there was no more consensus on the doctrines than when they began. If men had followed an ethical religion instead of the priestly religion of Catholic Rome or Presbyterian Geneva, there would have been no cause for such wars as disgraced the sixteenth and seventeenth centuries; for ethical religion unites men in brotherhood while priestly religion divides them into mutually hostile sects. Such is the indictment of the priestly type of religion.

ETHICS AS A RELIGION

Over against this type of religion, with its long-established prestige, its wide prevalence, its elaborate institutions, and its jealous guardianship of orthodox dogma against innovation or heresy, stands the prophetic type of religion. The two types have been in conflict ever since the first prophet arose to proclaim a new insight into the meaning of religion. The line of cleavage between the two types runs through all denominations, Catholic, Jewish and Protestant, dividing the men who would keep things as they are from those who, in Pastor John Robinson's words, expect "new light to break from God's word."

When we speak of prophets we think inevitably of the great figures of the Old Testament who stood forth to rebuke Israel for its neglect of divine law and its idolatries borrowed from the heathen tribes on its borders. We hear Isaiah thundering against the vain substitution of ritual for righteousness: "To what purpose is the multitude of your sacrifices unto me? saith the Lord: I am full of the burnt offerings of rams, and the fat of fed beasts. . . . Bring no more vain oblations; incense is an abomination unto me. . . . Your new moons and your appointed feasts my soul hateth. . . . Wash you, make you clean . . . cease to do evil; learn to do well; seek judgment, relieve the oppressed, judge the fatherless, plead for the widow." We hear Amos the shepherd of Tekoa: "I hate, I despise your feast days. . . . But let judgment roll down as waters, and righteousness as a mighty stream." We hear the prophet Micah: "What doth the

PRIESTLY AND PROPHETIC RELIGION

Lord require of thee, but to do justly, and to love mercy, and to walk humbly with thy God?"

Before these prophets appeared in Israel there had been some thinkers who had glimpses of the ethical import of religion. For example, as the late Professor James H. Breasted showed in his *The Dawn of Conscience,* the Egyptians left many moral precepts, like those of the scribe Ptah-Hotep. But the prophetic element in Egyptian religion was vitiated by the debasing worship of bulls, cats, crocodiles, jackals and other animals. Nor were any of the Egyptian gods comparable in dignity and righteousness with the one God of the Hebrews. It was the prophets of Israel who gave to the world the noble doctrine of ethical monotheism.

Here let it be said that the Hebrew prophet (*Nabi*) was not a prophet in our commonly accepted sense of the word. He was not a soothsayer or foreteller of events, but a forthspeaker of a message from Jehovah. His mission was to recall the people of Israel from their evil ways and proclaim the forgiveness of God for the repentant. No quarter was given to the idolatries camouflaged with ritual ceremonialism. "I have set thee ... to root out, and to pull down, and to destroy" was Jehovah's commission to Jeremiah. Short work was to be made of the idols.

The line of the Hebrew prophets culminated in Jesus of Nazareth. For near two thousand years his teachings have been the inspiration of prophetic religion. He spoke with authority and not as the scribes and the Pharisees.

ETHICS AS A RELIGION

His mortal enemies were the priestly masters of Jerusalem: mortal, because they finally brought him to his death on the cross by charging him before the Roman governor, Pilate, with the design of making himself king. Pilate "found no fault in him"; but "washed his hands" of the matter and allowed the execution to proceed. Though he was the inspirer of prophetic religion, Jesus himself was the victim of earlier prophesies. The Jews had for generations been expecting a messiah (anointed one) to deliver them from the yoke of Rome and restore the kingdom of David and Solomon. Several messianic passages in the Old Testament were applied to Jesus as his religious prestige grew, and he was hailed as the Messiah by his disciples and by the throngs that acclaimed him when he made his tragic entrance into Jerusalem. "We trusted that it had been he which should have redeemed Israel" was the mournful cry of disappointed disciples as they dispersed into Galilee after the crucifixion.

The accusation against Jesus of aspiring to be "king of the Jews" was simply ludicrous. He bore no resemblance to the zealots who from time to time had sought to rouse the Jews against the Roman Empire. He was completely indifferent to Rome. To a group who asked him if it was lawful to pay tribute to Caesar he answered, "Render to Caesar the things that are Caesar's, and to God the things that are God's." His kingdom was not of this world. He washed his hands of political questions, even as Pontius Pilate washed his of religious questions. Why, then, did he allow himself to be hailed as Messiah, when that title

PRIESTLY AND PROPHETIC RELIGION

was understood by his contemporaries to denote the long-awaited hero of the line of David who was to restore the political independence of Israel? This is a question to which the learned authors of the life of Jesus have sought various answers. To me the most satisfactory is a paradox: namely, that Jesus took the title of Messiah in order to put an end to the expectation of a political messiah. His view of his mission far transcended the task of the political liberation of Israel from the Roman yoke. He was concerned with the spiritual liberation of mankind from the yoke of sin. In a later chapter we shall see how Jesus, this wonderful preacher of prophetic religion, was transformed by the church into Christ the anointed king. It was the worst blow that religion ever received. *

Let us ask now what are the characteristic marks of prophetic religion as contrasted with priestly religion. In the first place the devotees of prophetic religion are free from the haunting suspicion that the discoveries of science or the speculations of philosophy might undermine their faith. Science does conflict with theology, as Andrew D. White has shown, because the theological systems of the past have presumed to trespass on the field of science by unverified pronouncements derived from Scripture. But theology is not religion; it is only the bungling attempt of scholars to define religion in the light of the knowledge

---

*An interesting modern parallel is the case of Gandhi. Vincent Sheean in his fascinating life of Gandhi, *Lead, Kindly Light,* has shown how embarrassing it was to the great Indian saint to be hailed with the title of Mahatma, or Great Soul. But he was powerless to prevent the people's enthusiastic acclaim.

ETHICS AS A RELIGION

available in their age and generation. Nor can the furthest reaches of man's intellect, whatever havoc it may make, and has made, with orthodox dogmas, ever abolish religion; because the utmost reaches of man's intellect cannot invalidate the experience of spiritual aspiration and satisfaction which is the hallmark of true religion.

Hence prophetic religion has no need of "ordained" or "consecrated" mediators. One of the basic tenets of Protestantism was the doctrine of the responsibility of the individual for his relations with God. Though it is still customary to speak of the "ordination" of a Protestant clergyman, the word has no such meaning as it has in priestly religion. For the minister does not become a special channel of divine grace, invested with quasi-magical power. He has the functions of preaching and pastoral cares. His parishioners may call upon him for spiritual advice or confide in him their errors; but he does not mete out penance to them. He may be summoned to the bedside of the dying to pray and console; but he does not administer the sacrament of extreme unction, the viaticum to speed the soul on its journey to "the undiscovered country from whose bourne no traveler returns." No masses are said for souls in purgatory. No saints are invoked as intercessors. The eucharist becomes a symbol in remembrance of the Last Supper of Jesus with his disciples, and not a re-enactment of his death. In short, prophetic religion dispenses with the very sacraments which are of prime importance in priestly religion. And it would be better to speak of the minister of the former type as "installed" or "inducted" rather than "ordained" or "consecrated."

Needless to say, ethical religion is of the prophetic type. It has faith in the as yet unappropriated power of men and women to rise "on stepping stones of their dead selves" to ever higher levels of character. Their responsibility is simple and direct. It cannot be avoided or delegated. To be sure, we may help one another in this search for righteous living; and such help is the best service that one can render to one's neighbor. But no one can supply merit for his neighbor or atone vicariously for his sin. Just as a man must himself take the nourishment which is needed for his physical life, so must he himself appropriate and assimilate his religion, which is his spiritual nourishment.

Unless men rise to this imperious responsibility there is little hope that the kingdom of God, which Jesus declared is "within you," will be realized on earth. Gerald W. Johnson in his recent book, *Our English Heritage,* has traced the rise of man to dignity and self-reliance in the modem centuries: "The stooping serf, himself a part of the real estate, straightening, slowly standing up, raising his eyes from the clod to the plant, to the flower, to the furrow, to the field beyond, at last to the face of the King. In the panel being woven now he stands erect and eyes the King with level gaze, and the King cannot gainsay him. What is the next panel to be? . . . We have no lack of pessimists who are certain that the work is beyond us. The development, they say, has come to its logical conclusion, the wheel has made its full turn, and retrogression is all that may be expected. The next panel that comes from the loom of Time, they prophesy, will show the level-eyed citizen beginning to quail before the glare of a dictator, beginning to stoop again, and to sink his gaze toward the earth."

From this dire fate one thing and one alone can save us —the revival of prophetic religion, the religion of ethics.

CHAPTER THREE

THE SEAT OF AUTHORITY IN RELIGION

Among the traits of human nature none seems more conspicuous or persistent than the desire of man to exercise authority over his fellow man. In politics this is the root of tyrannies, in economics of exploitation in social relations of caste and snobbery, in religion of hierarchies and heresy-hunting. It is the purpose of this chapter to inquire into the bases on which the assumption of authority in religion is founded, and to analyze the means and methods by which it is exercised.

We have seen in the preceding chapter how among primitive peoples some man, by virtue of a commanding personality, gained a reputation of enjoying a special relation to the mysterious powers which controlled men's lives. He alone interpreted the will of these powers, prescribed the ceremonies and sacrifices to win their favor or avoid their wrath, and provided the magic "medicine" which healed men's diseases and kept them obedient to the taboos on their behavior. In this primitive exercise of authority may we not see foreshadowed the oracle of Delphi, the Roman augurs, the medieval hierarchy, the Puritan theocracy, and papal infallibility?

The sources on which the various religious denominations base their claims to authority are many and diverse. For the Jews, of course, the fundamental source is the Torah, the Mosaic Law. According to the account in Genesis the law was handed down by Jehovah to Moses on Mount Sinai, on tablets of stone. It prohibited the worship of any god in preference to Jehovah, or of any idols. It forbade the taking of God's name in vain (oaths) and enjoined the strict observance of the Sabbath. It prescribed the honoring of one's parents as the condition for a long life. And in the last five commandments (the "second table") it issued its "thou shalt nots" against murder, theft, adultery, perjury and covetousness. The Ten Commandments thus combined the ceremonial concept of the worship of one supreme God with the prescription of ethical conduct. They laid the foundation for the religion of ethical monotheism—a marked advance over any previous religion in the world, and the germ of all the higher religions that were to follow.

The Torah was expounded and expanded by the scribes and Pharisees in involved commentaries, not always edifying. The priestly family of Levi later became its guardians and the masters of its ceremonies. The prophets defended its sanctity against the idolatrous encroachments of the heathen nations bordering on Palestine. The central idea in the Hebrew religion was the covenant between Jehovah and his people. Though they fell away again and again from the observance of his law, yet there would always be a "saving remnant" to deserve the fulfillment of the covenant. Though the foreigner might reduce the nation to servitude, a deliverer (messiah) would come to restore the kingdom of David and Solomon. And in the end all the nations would be gathered to the holy hill of Zion.

The Jews (at least the orthodox Jews) have never abandoned this belief that their race is the "chosen people" of God. It has persisted through centuries of obloquy and persecution. It has been held in a far more serious sense than the American Philistine's boast that this is "God's own country." Even the distinguished liberal professor of the University of Jerusalem, Joseph Klausner (incidentally, the author of the best life of Jesus), says in his recent book, *From Jesus to Paul*. "We Jews hope and expect that the time shall come when the prayer which we pray three times daily, the 'Alenu' prayer, shall be realized, and the Kingdom of Heaven in the Jewish sense of ethical monotheism shall be established in the world, and the politico-spiritual Messianic ideal of Israel shall also be realized in all its fullness, and the Jewish people shall dwell in their historic national land, and shall speak their national tongue, and shall continue to develop their historic national culture in the spirit of their prophets and their sages. Then, of course, much shall be changed in the ceremonial laws of Judaism, although they shall not be altogether abolished, since they serve to protect the existence of the nation. . . . And Judaism in the form of ethico-prophetic monotheism shall spread over all the world."

Religion owes a great debt to the Hebrews, especially to the Hebrew prophets; but they vitiated the doctrine of ethical monotheism by their equal insistence on the doctrine of Israel as the chosen people of God. This emphasis, effective as it has been through the centuries in preserving their solidarity in spite of dispersion and persecution, nevertheless set them apart from the main current of religious thought. Jesus had transcended the particularism of the Law by his teaching of universalism. He had mortally offended the scribes and Pharisees by setting his "But I say unto you" against the ritualistic injunctions and prohibitions. But his amendments were rejected, and he paid the price for his heretical boldness. Judaism will continue to revere the religion of its fathers and celebrate its feasts; but there is little prospect that all the nations of the world will be gathered to the holy hill of Zion. Messianic hopes have faded away. The religion of the future, the only religion worthy of a man's devotion, must be free from the trammels of racialism, ritualism and legalism. It must be a universal religion to meet the unlimited and illimitable aspirations of man for spiritual growth.

Roman Catholicism puts forth the claim to be just that kind of religion. The word "catholic" means universal; and just as Judaism has foretold the gathering of all the nations to Zion, so Catholicism insists that all the dissenting sects will eventually be gathered into the one true church, that there may be "one fold and one shepherd." The foundation on which the Catholic Church rests its claim to universal religious authority is four-fold in nature: namely, the Bible, the Writings of the church fathers, the decrees of the church councils, and the pronouncements of the hierarchy culminating in the infallible pope, bishop of Rome. Of these authorities the last is paramount. And the warrant for this tremendous power of the pope is found in a passage in the sixteenth chapter of the Gospel of Matthew—though the passage is of dubious authenticity. It is Jesus' alleged commission to the apostle Peter to exercise on earth the power of heaven: "And I say also unto thee, that thou art Peter, and upon this rock *[petra]* I will build my church; and the gates of hell shall not prevail against it. And I will give unto thee the keys of the kingdom of heaven: and whatsoever thou shalt bind on earth shall be bound in heaven: and whatsoever thou shalt loose on earth shall be loosed in heaven." (The keys of heaven are emblazoned on the papal arms.)

Now Peter, according to the teaching of the church, went to Rome and became the first bishop there, from whom the line of popes has descended by "apostolic succession" to our own day. The painted medallions of them can be seen running like a frieze around the gallery of the church of St. Paul Without the Walls in Rome. The mother church of Christendom was named for St. Peter; and around the base of its lofty dome, in letters of gold on a blue background, runs the Latin inscription *"Tu es Petrus, et super hanc petram aedificabo ecclesiam meant, et portae injeri non prevalebunt contra earn."* Two other passages from the New Testament are cited to confirm the primacy of Peter among the apostles, albeit he was the disciple who denied Jesus at the trial. The first (Luke 22:31-32) reads: "Simon, Simon, behold, Satan hath desired to have you, that he may sift you as wheat: but I have prayed for thee, that thy faith fail not: and when thou art converted, strengthen thy brethren." And the second (John 21:15-17) was a triple injunction to Peter to "feed my sheep."

In spite of the use of the above passages to vindicate the special standing of Peter among the disciples of Jesus, and the abundant citations from Scripture in the bulls and encyclicals of the popes, the Bible is far less an authority than the church in the Catholic religion. The great St. Augustine of Hippo, whose writings dominated the theology of the Middle Ages, said flatly: "I would not believe the Scriptures unless moved thereto by the authority of the holy church." Nor does the church allow the laity to "search the Scriptures," to find the way to salvation, by placing the Bible in the hands of the people. It is enough for the laity to take its instructions from and render its obedience to the priest.

In the early centuries of Christianity the church councils decided questions of doctrine by the free vote of the prelates summoned from all parts of Christendom. But as the power of the popes grew rapidly after the fourth century they tended to dictate to the councils, and even in some instances annulled their decrees. This practice reached its peak at the great Council of Trent in the sixteenth century, which, like all the councils, was supposed to be guided by the Holy Ghost, but which in reality was run by the pope. As a cynical historian put it, "The Holy Ghost came to Trent every day in the mail-bag from Rome." Trent was the last of the ecumenical (all world) councils. Since then even the gesture of summoning the prelates of Christendom to deliberate on doctrine has been abandoned. Ecumenical councils yielded to Vatican councils, and the last of these in 1869-70, by decreeing the infallibility of the pope, put an end to any further need for councils of any sort. The pope's word was final. *Roma locuta, causa finita est.*

The Protestant revolt from Rome shifted the seat of authority in religion. All the reformers—Luther, Calvin, Zwingli, Knox, Cranmer—clung tenaciously to the fundamental doctrines of the church: the creation of the world in six days, the corruption of man through Adam's fall, the salvation of the elect through the vicarious atonement of Christ, the day of judgment, and the reception of the saved into a heaven of eternal bliss, with the condemnation of the lost to a hell of eternal torment. But they rejected the authority of the Catholic Church in the application of the doctrines. They repudiated the pope, denouncing him as anti-Christ; they abolished the confessional and the sacraments of penance and extreme unction, and changed the significance of the rest. They did away with purgatory and the intercession of the Virgin Mary and the saints. They left man face to face with God, without priestly mediation.

For the authority of the church the reformers substituted the authority of the Bible. The inspired Scriptures, and they alone, contained all that was necessary for salvation. Hence the reformers put the Bible into the hands of the people, translating it from Latin and Greek into the modem languages, so that "the plowman might read it when following the furrow and the weaver while at his loom." Cotton Mather, outlining the curriculum for Harvard College, urged the students to "lay Christ in the bottom" of their work through the study of the sacred texts. Courses in Hebrew and Greek were required. It was not till 1801 that students were allowed to substitute French for Hebrew at the request of their parents or guardians; and not till the closing years of the nineteenth century that a science might be substituted for Greek in the entrance requirements. Every college founded in the eighteenth century, except Franklin's University of Pennsylvania, was primarily a religious institution (as are most of the so-called "fresh-water" colleges today); and prior to the American Revolution the great majority of the students entered the ministry. The college presidents were generally clergymen who combined with their executive duties the professorship of Christian evidences. The coincidence of laymen serving as presidents of the four universities of Harvard, Yale, Princeton and Columbia falls within my own memory.

This virtual monopoly of education for the service of religion was of course due to the emphasis which Protestantism put on the Bible and on the "call" to teach the truths of the Bible. Preaching became the chief duty of the Protestant minister, whereas it was secondary to ceremonial rites in the Catholic Church. And because God might at any time elect any man to preach his word, it was necessary to have an educated ministry. If a man were called to be a vessel of grace, the vessel must overflow grammatically. It was only in the crude regions of the frontier that education was deemed unnecessary for the preacher—and even detrimental to his faith.

Though all the Protestant sects agreed on the final authority of the Bible as against that of the church, they differed widely in their interpretation of the Bible. For the fundamentalists every word of the Bible was divinely inspired. The writers, in the words of an early church father, were the "amanuenses of the Holy Ghost." When

ETHICS AS A RELIGION

Mr. Bryan was asked at the Dayton trial whether he believed that Jonah was swallowed by a great fish, he replied, "I believe it if it is in the Bible"—which it was. On the other hand, Martin Luther, the father of Protestantism, frankly rejected the Epistle of James, calling it an "epistle of straw" because it declared that "faith without works is dead." For Luther only that part of the Bible which contained the doctrine of justification by faith in Christ was inspired. Furthermore, since the Bible offered so many possibilities of interpretation, a great number of sects arose, each finding in the Bible the authority for its belief and practice. The Baptists cited scriptural authority for the practice of immersion; the Methodists for the doctrine of the perseverance of the saints; the Episcopalians for the institution of bishops; the Presbyterians and Lutherans for church government by presbyteries and synods; the Congregationalists for the independence of each congregation. The Roman Catholic Church, with its authority firmly established in the hierarchy, regards the repudiation of Rome as the great heresy, and has constantly maintained the doctrine that the dissenting sects would return eventually to allegiance to the mother church.

Now the contributions of the Hebrew prophets, the Catholic hierarchy and the Protestant reformers to the spiritual development of the Western world have been many and great. The Hebrew doctrine of ethical monotheism was, as we have said, the foundation for all the higher religions. During the Dark Ages the Roman

Church not only preserved what it could of the learning of antiquity but mitigated the harshness of the endemic feudal wars. And from their direct access to the Bible the Protestant sects drew spiritual nourishment and a heightened sense of religious responsibility. Ethical religion recognizes these contributions, and yet cannot find the seat of religious authority in the Jewish Law or the Catholic Church or the Holy Bible. For it the sole authority lies in the human breast. "Creeds," said Emerson, "are a disease of the intellect." Nothing, he declared, was at last sacred to man but the promptings of his own conscience. That it is which teaches him to love the right and shun the wrong. The law inscribed in his heart, as the ancient prophet said, is holier than any law handed down by tradition. It is not the church that makes people good, but good people that make the church.

Moreover, the voice of conscience is the only authority that can furnish a man with a convincing reason why he should cleave to the right and eschew the wrong. Law, church, Scripture all impose their injunctions, but only the mandate which comes from the heart of man himself deserves to be called "authority" for him. I was once walking home from a meeting with a young man who said to me, "Why should I be ethical? I am free to do as I choose. Why should I not indulge my appetites, feather my nest, and prosper even at the expense of my neighbor?" It would have been futile to answer that he was forbidden to do wrong by the church or the Bible; for they meant nothing to him. The only effective appeal was

ETHICS AS A RELIGION

to his own sense of responsibility to society and to the better promptings of his own nature. Self-discipline is the only true discipline for free men. Where outward compulsion begins freedom ends. When Portia told Shylock that he must show mercy to the merchant of Venice, he replied, "On what compulsion must I tell me that." He had the law on his side. He had his bond calling for the pound of flesh. But Portia's answer, in one of the most magnificent passages of Shakespeare, declared that mercy was above the "sceptered sway" of kings and "enthroned in the hearts of men." "Look within," said the emperor-philosopher Marcus Aurelius; "there is the source of virtue." And the philosopher-poet Browning wrote:

Truth is within ourselves; it takes no rise
From outward things, whatever you may believe.
There is a source and center in us all
Where truth abides in fulness.

"Authority" in common parlance means the right and power of a man or state to exact obedience to dictates and laws. But literally the word has quite a different meaning. It is from the Latin *augeo,* which signifies to "enlarge" or "increase," and which furnishes us with such words as "augment" and "auction." Whatever, therefore, enlarges a man's spiritual vision and increases his moral strength is for him religious authority. Growth, not profession, is the test of a man's religion; and growth in character is the measure of that internal authority which bids him strive for moral perfection. Obedience to this authority, which is akin to what Quakers call the "inner light," is the chief duty of man.

In a recent symposium on the subject of religious education I advocated the ethical conception of the duty and the competence of man to acknowledge the religious authority provided by his own conscience. A priest interrupted me courteously with the remark, "But yours is a man-made religion." "Of course it is," I replied, "and so is every religion that men have professed throughout the ages." Man did not make the sun and the stars; but he has been the creator of every idea and every institution that the world has ever known. The Catholic Church, as well as the Ethical Society, is "man-made." Even the assumption that Jesus established the church (an assumption that finds little support in the Gospels) is a human conception. And every ascription of authority to Torah, church or Scripture is made by the human mind. There are mysteries, of course, which are beyond the grasp of the human mind, but they cannot be religious authorities for a man, because they do not "enlarge" his spiritual vision. He cannot obey what he cannot comprehend. But what he can comprehend, and is therefore bound to obey, is the voice of conscience in his own breast. There, and only there, is the seat of authority in ethical religion.

CHAPTER FOUR

ETHICAL RELIGION AND CHRISTIANITY

SOME YEARS AGO I attended a series of lectures by the distinguished church historian Adolf Harnack in the Great Hall of the University of Berlin. The subject of Harnack's lectures was "Das Wesen des Christentums," and this title was translated in the English publication as "What Is Christianity?" But the translation might better have been "The Essence of Christianity," for the word *"Wesen"* has a positive content, meaning the very core or kernel of a thing.

Hamack summed up the essential meaning of Christianity in three articles: namely, the fatherhood of God, the infinite worth of every human soul, and the doctrine of the kingdom of heaven. He had ample justification for these propositions in the Gospels. The first words of the prayer which Jesus taught his disciples were "Our Father," and the father image is constantly used in the Gospels to designate the relation of God to man. In the most beautiful parables of Jesus it is a father who welcomes with rejoicing the return of his prodigal son. Again, the infinite worth of the individual is illustrated in the parable of the lost sheep, for which the shepherd will not give up the search until it is found and returned to the fold. And finally, the kingdom of heaven was the phrase constantly used by Jesus to denote the eventual triumph of the rule of love and righteousness in the heart of man. "The kingdom of God is within you."

Yet, although Hamack's three propositions were all essentials of Christianity, none of them was exclusively Christian. In ancient Egypt the reforming Pharaoh Ikhnaton had proclaimed one God, the father of men; and the Hebrew prophets had defended the same doctrine against the paganism of the surrounding tribes. The Stoic philosophers had taught that every man had in him a spark of divinity—what a contrast to the church's doctrine of human depravity! And before Jesus had begun his min-

ETHICS AS A RELIGION

istry, the Roman poet Vergil, in his Fourth Eclogue, had prophesied a veritable kingdom of heaven, when all evil should be banished from the earth. Granted in the teaching of Jesus these doctrines were presented with the incomparable persuasiveness of his personal example, we cannot in all fairness concede that they were original with him. Nor can we overlook the fact that Jesus was indifferent to some problems which have, or ought to have, religious significance for us. As an inhabitant of an inconspicuous province of the Roman Empire, he apparently showed no interest in political morality and refused to debate with his disciples the justice or injustice of submitting to Caesar's authority. Though he was a welcome guest at many houses, he treated his own family with marked indifference. One incident recorded in the synoptic Gospels seems almost cruel: "While he yet talked to the people, behold, his mother and his brethren stood without, desiring to speak with him. . . . But he answered . . . Who is my mother? and who are my brethren? And he stretched forth his hand toward his disciples, and said, Behold my mother and my brethren! For whosoever shall do the will of my Father which is in heaven, the same is my brother, and sister, and mother."

So far in this chapter we have used the word "Christianity" as a synonym for the teaching of Jesus; and if it had so remained this world might have been a paradise instead of the awful mess which greed, unholy ambition, hatred and war have made it. For Jesus taught humility, love and peace. But not long after his death philosophers, theologians and priests began to transform the simple gospel which he preached into elaborate creeds and ceremonies which he would have found as alien to his spirit as the Hebrew prophets before him had found the worship of Baal. They mingled Greek metaphysics with oriental mysticism, borrowing unintelligible terms from a debased Platonism, importing the idea of a trinity of gods from Babylon and Egypt, disputing fiercely and often with bloodshed over the question whether the Son was of the same substance or only of like substance with the Father. In short, they substituted the Christ of the church for the Jesus of the Gospels. For Jesus himself knew nothing of these subtleties of argument. He never (except in the doubtful passage in Matthew) spoke of a church or a triune God. He never mentioned the fall of Adam. His test for entrance into the kingdom of heaven was a purely ethical one: to love God and to do unto men as you would have them do unto you. He was not a theologian but an exemplar of righteousness.

It was St. Paul who established the church. This remarkable man was a strange mixture of weakness and strength. Small of stature, a sufferer from epilepsy, he was yet a man of amazing zeal and endurance. He traveled ceaselessly, founding churches from Asia Minor to Rome, and Writing them letters of exhortation and reproof to keep them faithful to their Christian profession. In his first letter to the Corinthians he could write the most beautiful panegyric on love (Chapter 13) and follow it (Chapter 15) with a painfully feeble argument to prove the resurrection of the body. Born in the cosmopolitan city of Tarsus in Asia Minor and educated at the feet of the distinguished rabbi Gamaliel, he was, in his own words, "a Hebrew of the Hebrews," and a zealous defender of the Mosaic Law. He persecuted the followers of Jesus in his early manhood, and was a consenting witness to the stoning of the first Christian martyr, Stephen. While on his way to Damascus to exterminate the group of Christians there, he was stricken from his horse by a blinding light and heard a voice saying: "Saul, Saul, why persecutest thou me?" From that time he became as zealous a promoter of Christianity as he had been of Judaism. The sufferings which he endured on his missionary journeys —scourging, imprisonment, shipwreck, attempted assassination—are told in his letters and in the Acts of the Apostles.

It was the death of Jesus on the cross, and not his life in Galilee and Judea, that interested Paul and became the central theme of his theology. "I am resolved," he wrote, "to know nothing among you but Jesus Christ and him crucified." He may or may not have met Jesus "in the flesh"; but if he did, he never mentions Jesus' parables nor refers to the episodes in Jesus' career. We must remember that all of Paul's epistles were written and he himself was dead before the oldest (Mark) of the written Gospels appeared, although the Gospels precede the Epistles in the canon of the New Testament. For Paul, as for Jesus, "Scripture" meant the Old Testament.

Paul was not only the pioneer founder of churches, but

he was also the first formulator of the doctrine, held ever afterwards by both Catholics and orthodox Protestants, of the utter corruption of man and his redemption only by the blood of Christ. "For as in Adam all die, even so in Christ shall all be made alive." This dismal doctrine of "original sin" was no part of the teaching of Jesus. He recognized, as we all do, that men stray from the path of righteousness; but he believed that men have the ability to regain the path. It was "when he *came to himself*' that the prodigal son returned to his father's house. Repentance alone was necessary. "Go and sin no more" was Jesus' command to the erring. "Be ye perfect even as your father in heaven is perfect" was the standard which he set up for humanity. Could he have spoken thus to men cursed from birth with the fatal impotence to take a single step toward righteousness of their own will? No; the theologians perverted the teachings of Jesus and crucified him anew. Instead of seeking to understand and apply his moral commands, they wrangled over his "substance" and "person," outlawing their fellow theologians who disagreed with them, and imposing the majority (orthodox) opinion on the church by the power of the state. At the great Council of Nicaea (325), where the doctrine of the Trinity was made binding on the church, the Emperor Constantine sat enthroned between two bishops, sanctioning the doctrine and assuming the title "isapostolos," the equal of the apostles.

And this brings us to a second transformation that Christianity underwent in the early centuries. Not only

ETHICS AS A RELIGION

was the Jesus of the Gospels supplanted by the Christ of the church, but the unholy alliance between the Christian church and the political state was made. Up to the fourth century of our era the Christians were cruelly persecuted by the state because they refused to recognize the gods of Rome or to burn incense at the altars of the divine Caesar. Still they grew in numbers and influence, for the blood of the martyrs was the seed of the church. They even gained adherents in Caesar's household, until the church father Tertullian could say in his *Apology* to the emperor: "We fill your camps and your forums." In the year 311, as we have noted, the Emperor Galerius gave the Christians the right to practice their religion without penalty. Two years later Constantine the Great adopted Christianity as the official religion of the Roman Empire. And a few years later the Emperor Theodosius published a code of laws visiting with heavy penalties any who should continue to worship the old gods of Rome. Thus Christianity passed through four phases in its relation to the state. First it was outlawed, then permitted, then made official, then prescribed as the only religion permitted.

This complete reversal of the relations between the church and the imperial state was of tremendous importance for Christianity. The church became wealthy; for Constantine endowed it liberally with lands and buildings. It became worldly, engrossed largely in managing its increasing possessions. The clergy became a favored class, and the prelates often reveled in luxury. "Make me a bishop, and I will forthwith become a Christian," wrote

ETHICAL RELIGION AND CHRISTIANITY

a cynical pagan. It is said that the Renaissance Pope Leo X ascended the throne of St. Peter with the remark, "We intend to enjoy this pontificate." The extent to which these mundane concerns penetrated the church is shown by the repeated attempts of reformers (Hildebrand, Francis of Assisi, Loyola, Luther) to restore it to its primitive purity.

The sinister alliance between throne and altar often gave divine sanction to the misrule of despots and political support to the mandates of the church.* It is nonsense to speak of the "conversion" of Constantine to Christianity. He was no more of a Christian than was Attila the Hun. He was a wicked, cruel man who did not stop at the murder of his own son. His adoption of Christianity as the state religion was a matter of pure political expediency. The Christians had grown so rapidly that they were a force to be reckoned with. The famous Edict of Milan (313) reads: "We have resolved to grant to Christians as well as to all others the liberty to practice the religion they prefer, in order that whatever exists of dignity or power [in Christianity] may help and favor us and all who are under our government." The last phrase reveals the emperor's purpose. He simply wanted "what-

---

* The history of the countries of Europe in which the church has been a prominent political influence is filled with compacts and concordats between the state and the church. Note the bargain between Napoleon and Pope Pius VII in the concordat of 1801 and the more recent Lateran treaty of 1929 between Mussolini and Pope Pius XI, by which the unspeakable Mussolini was recognized by the pope and in turn recognized the pope as sovereign over the tiny Vatican state.

ever power" there was in Christianity on his side. Legend has it that, being hard pressed in a battle, Constantine saw a cross in the sky with the words "In this sign conquer"; and forthwith vowed that if he won the battle he would adopt the cross instead of the laburnum as the standard of Rome. But we need no legend to explain Constantine's act. He saw in the cross not a symbol of salvation but a political fetish. He hoped that its worship would "help and favor" his imperial fortunes.

In addition to the invasion of theological systems based on Greek metaphysics and the rise of the church as a political power, Christianity underwent other transformations in its early centuries. It had conquered the pagan religion of Rome, to be sure, but only at the expense of absorbing some of the features of that religion. The Roman basilicas were turned into Christian churches and Christian priests took the place of the Roman augurs. Many of the ceremonials of the old religion, especially those derived from the Etruscans, were introduced into the church, such as the *sedia gestatoria* or throne on which the pope was carried on solemn occasions and the kissing of the toe of the bronze statue of St. Peter. The dogma as well as the ritual of the church was hardened into a system which dominated the Middle Ages and which is still preserved in its entirety by the Catholic Church. *Eostre* was a Teutonic festival celebrating the awakening of nature in spring. It was adopted as the chief festival of the church (Easter), celebrating the resurrection of Christ. The resurrection story itself had parallels in a number of Eastern legends of heroes raised from the dead.

Most important, however, and I think most unfortunate of all the transformations of primitive Christianity was the elevation of Jesus to the position of an oriental monarch to be bowed down to. Holden's famous hymn "Coronation" is sung in thousands of churches today:

> *All hail the power of Jesus' name;*
> *Let angels prostrate fall;*
> *Bring forth the royal diadem*
> *To crown him Lord of all.*

There is no warrant for such language in the Gospels. Jesus never spoke of himself as a monarch or demanded homage. He was, in his own words, the way, the truth, the life, the light, the vine, the good shepherd. He rebuked those who would worship him, declaring himself to be subject to his father God. The phrase "son of man," so often used by him, means in the original Aramaic simply "man." If anyone had offered to put a "royal diadem" on his head, he would have put it aside more resolutely than Julius Caesar did. The only crown that he ever wore was a crown of thorns. To deify Jesus, as the church has done, is to substitute a "second person" in an unintelligible Trinity for a marvelous living personality.

Now the creeds of Christendom are all affected with the aforesaid encumbrances of metaphysics, miracle and mystery. The priests and the (orthodox) ministers are pledged to accept them and to preach them to their congregations. The oldest of the creeds, the Apostles' Creed, was a baptismal formula prescribed for entrance into the community of believers, and it is repeated Sunday after Sunday in thousands of churches. How many of the worshipers really believe in their hearts such phrases of the creed as he "was conceived by the Holy Ghost and born of the Virgin Mary," "he descended into hell," "on the third day he rose and ascended into heaven," we do not know. Furthermore, the word "Christian" is used loosely. Men speak of America as a Christian country. That could mean either that the great majority of the people of America are professing Christians or that the government recognizes Christianity as the religion of the state. But neither of these things is true. Statistics show that 56 per cent of the population have no religious affiliation; and the First Amendment to the Constitution declared that the government had no part in sponsoring or supporting Christianity or any other religion. As early as Washington's day this principle was affirmed in a treaty negotiated with the Barbary state of Tripoli in 1796. It states:

> As the government of the United States of America is not in any sense founded on the Christian religion; as it has in itself no character of enmity against the laws, religion, or tranquillity of Musselmen ... it is declared by the parties that no pretext arising from religious opinions shall ever produce an interruption of the harmony existing between the two countries.

ETHICAL RELIGION AND CHRISTIANITY

The word "Christian" is also used loosely in regard to individuals. An upright man is often called a Christian, although he may not believe a single article of the creed. Abraham Lincoln was claimed by every denomination, even the Catholics, after his death. But he belonged to none. He said in reply to a friend who asked him why he had never joined a church, "If I found a church whose only requirement for membership was love of God and one's neighbor, I would join it willingly." But there was no such church.

Being just, kind, humble and truthful does not make a man a Christian. I once knew such a man, and when I asked a Presbyterian minister how he could accept a creed which condemned my friend to eternal punishment, he replied, "I consider Mr. X. an unconscious Christian." But Mr. X. was a conscious non-Christian, and the clergyman knew it. What other profession tempts so much to sophistry and evasion!

Ethical religion is free of all this theological apologetic. As Christian in *Pilgrim's Progress* feels the burden of sin roll off his shoulders when he reaches the Gate Beautiful, so does the follower of Ethical Society shed all the paraphernalia of ritual and creed. Nor does he in so doing "throw out the child with the bath." He retains a faith as firm as any founded on the creeds of Christendom. These creeds represent the faith of men of long centuries past, men who, however sincere in their religion, yet knew little or nothing of modem science. They abound in misconceptions of chronology, geography, astronomy and human psychology. Men of today are infinitely better prepared to formulate their religion than were the Nicene fathers of the fourth century or the Westminster divines of the seventeenth century. Yet the church clings to these antiquated and embarrassing symbols, and tries to square them with the insights of today. Nowhere except in religion do we make the past our jailer, "hoarding it in musty parchments." "I fear this iron yoke of conformity hath left a slavish print upon our necks," wrote John Milton in the *Areopagitica.*

The chief end of man according to the Westminster Shorter Catechism is "to glorify God and enjoy him forever." But the phrase "to glorify God" is without positive meaning. What glory can a mortal man confer upon a being of acknowledged perfection? Surely the worship of God does not add to his glory. The chief end of man, we submit, is his own progress in the knowledge, love and practice of the right. For what do any of the great religions aim at but the moral improvement of mankind? If for some persons incense, candles and genuflections help in the process, well and good. For other persons they are superfluities or even superstitions. Are not forms of worship largely matters of the individual's aesthetic taste? Emerson left the ministry because his conscience would not allow him to' administer the eucharist as the body and blood of Christ or to pray in public every Sunday morning at eleven o'clock. His fellow townsman Thoreau declared that the orthodox Christian could not understand Jesus.

ETHICAL RELIGION AND CHRISTIANITY

I am well aware that too many readers (if there be many) this chapter will be regarded as an attack on Christianity. But such is not the purpose of the writer. He yields to no one in his reverence for the great prophet of Galilee, who raised to higher levels every life that he touched, showing the way to righteousness and peace. But the church has not followed his precepts and example. Permeated by metaphysical subtleties, Roman legalism, medieval monasticism and modem materialism, it has conformed to the secular patterns of the age. This is not an indictment brought by an enemy of Christianity, but a condition recognized by many prominent church leaders. Henry K. Sherrill, presiding bishop of the Episcopal Church, declared at the triennial convention of the church at San Francisco on September 26, 1949, that the Christian church had become "little more than a pale reflection of contemporary society." "We are all," he continued, "too conservative, too limited, and let us say frankly without any gross interpretation of the word, too worldly." Was the bishop "attacking" Christianity? Was he not rather confessing, if unwittingly, that the Christian church in all these centuries had not been successful in winning the world? The fundamentalists of every creed are waging a losing battle to preserve the Pauline-Augustinian-Calvinistic scheme of salvation as the divinely revealed purpose of God. The liberal Christians are intent on saving as much as they can of traditional theology by apologetics and allegory. While the half of our people who are unchurched, along with we know not how many nominally connected with the churches, are in a state of spiritual confusion,

> *Wandering between two worlds, one dead,*
> *The other powerless to be born.*

We face this distressful situation with a religious faith which we confidently believe can inspire men and women with all the zeal for righteous living that the theologies of the past have claimed to be derived alone from their doctrines, and which can bring that poise and peace to the human heart which is the condition of a free and integrated personality. We strive to recommend this faith in a spirit of humility and sympathy. It is by quiet persuasion, not by coercion, intimidation, denunciation or scornful innuendo that truth must be advanced. I emphasize the *irenic* nature of our dissension from traditional Christianity because of an incident which happened recently. A candidate for a doctor's degree in a Catholic university chose as the subject of his dissertation the philosophy and aims of the Ethical Societies. In the course of it he indulged in vituperation of the leaders of the societies as animated by a hatred of Christianity. How he could have deduced from the writings and addresses of Felix Adler, William Salter, Horace Bridges and the rest, from the works which abound in testimony to the debt we owe to the superb moral teachings of Jesus, such a monstrous misrepresentation of our position can only be explained by that "fatal twist" which Mark Twain said affects men with a sacerdotal training. Judgments passed on others are often more of a revelation of the man who makes the judgment than of the man who is judged. In imputing hatred to us could the young man have been revealing his own attitude toward those who do not accept the particular brand of religion which he had been taught to believe was fixed, final and synonymous with religion itself?

The remedy often proposed for the plight in which the churches find themselves is a return to primitive Christianity. But we cannot return to primitive things. Humanity moves forward. Nor is it true to say that Christianity "has never been tried." It has been tried for nineteen centuries in the Western world called "Christendom"; and we live in a world today disgraced by strife, oppression, fear, war and the rumors of war. A bishop appears in khaki. The same ship ironically carries in its hold munitions to kill men and on its deck Red Cross nurses to save men. Of course, Christianity is not responsible for creating this reign of hatred and carnage—though in the past it has launched cruel persecutions and bitter wars. The charge against it is that it has not been able to prevent these barbarities. Christianity, to paraphrase the dying words of Edith Cavell, "is not enough." We need a new religion: a religion which shall fulfill the dreams of the prophets of righteousness from Amos and Isaiah and Jesus and St. Francis to Emerson and Adler and Schweitzer; a religion which shall satisfy the intellect as well as uplift the soul; a religion which is free of every trace of sophistry, apologetics and cant; a religion which aban-

ETHICS AS A RELIGION

dons the futile search for answers to insoluble theological riddles; a religion which centers its interest in man and puts its trust in the capacity of man to rise by his untiring moral endeavor to ever higher levels of life. We have had more than enough of theology. Thomas Huxley said that the word reminded him of quack medicine. What the world needs is a religion of humanity. And what a force for the redemption of the world from the hell of inhumanity into which it has fallen could be exerted by the churches, with their numbers and wealth, if they would frankly abandon their outdated creeds and devote all their energies to the understanding and improvement of the nature of man and his institutions.

The clergy are constantly bemoaning the fact that men have lost faith in God. Our complaint is that they have never acquired faith in man. They have been taught for centuries that man has been condemned by Adam's fall to a ruin from which he can be saved only by belief in the vicarious sacrifice of Christ. We need no pope or bishop or revivalist to tell us that men sin. The evidence is abundant on every hand. But the evil that they do is of themselves, and not because Adam ate a forbidden apple in the Garden of Eden. And they must work out their redemption for themselves. The church is right in its diagnosis, but not in its therapeutic. Instead of discouraging men and frightening them by dwelling on their impotence, the religious teachers should, like Jesus himself, encourage them by the recognition and cultivation of the potentialities for good that are latent in human nature. For these potentialities exist as truly as the impulses to evil. It is from the heart of man that the insights precede which inspire him to attain his true stature as a "son of God."

> *All that hath been majestical*
> *In life or death since time began*
> *Is native in the simple heart of all,*
> *The angel heart of man.*

CHAPTER FIVE

INTELLECTUAL PIETY

Among the Christians of the earliest centuries there circulated a number of writings in the form of gospels, epistles and apocalypses, bearing the names of the apostles or their associates: such as the Gospel of Peter, the Epistle of Barnabas, the Gospel of the Hebrews, the Acts of Paul, the Apocalypse of Peter, and so forth. These writings were read in private and in the congregations for edification. The authors (mostly unknown to us), claiming the gift of the Holy Spirit which Jesus had said would descend upon his followers, were free to write as the spirit moved them. It was not until the close of the fourth century that the church excluded these prophecies and homilies from the "canon" of the New Testament: that is, from the list of the authorized Gospels and Epistles which were to be accepted as the authentic writings of the apostles of Christ, including St. Paul. Even then, however, "canonical" and "apostolic" were not strictly synonymous terms. For example, the Epistle to the Hebrews which is included in the canon was not written by Paul; the Eastern Church never accepted the book of Revelations as the work of the apostle John; and Martin Luther rejected the Epistle of James as a "worthless epistle of straw."

One of the earliest and most influential writers of the literature of Christian edification was a certain Clement of Alexandria, sometimes called the first Christian philosopher. In his "homilies" or sermons Clement wrote: "Our Master said, 'Be honest brokers.' " There is no record of such a saying of Jesus in our Gospels; but that need not surprise us, for the literature of edification contains many an alleged remark of Jesus handed down by tradition. But what was the meaning of this strange command of Jesus as reported by Clement, "Be honest brokers"? Of course it had no reference to the stock market. Could it have been suggested by the incident of the money-changers in the temple? But Clement was writing for the ordinary members of the Christian congregation, addressing them as "brokers." In the Century Dictionary the word "broker" is defined as follows: "A middleman or agent who negotiates for others the purchase or sale of stocks, bonds, commodities or properties of any kind." There are not only money brokers, but cotton brokers, coffee brokers, real estate brokers, etc. The marriage broker was a figure of the Far East, as we find him in Puccini's opera *Madame Butterfly*. And perhaps the most unusual application of the word is in a passage of the essayist Addison: "Tom Folio is a broker in learning, employed to get together good editions and stock the libraries of great men." So there is what might be called an intellectual or spiritual brokerage. The teacher, for example, is an intellectual broker or middleman, mediating to his pupils the values of their cultural heritage. The clergyman is a religious broker, furnishing spiritual guidance and comfort for his congregation. The true statesman is a political broker, adjusting the inherited compulsions of a past generation to the ever changing needs of an evolutionary society. Nor is this function of brokerage confined to professional men only. Each one of us, by virtue of our share in community interests, is necessarily involved in the task of examining, evaluating, and either supporting or combating the movements which are clamoring for disciples in our complex and bewildering society. To you and me, therefore, the command is addressed: "Be honest brokers." Now, intellectual piety is nothing more nor less than

INTELLECTUAL PIETY

the honest brokerage of the mind discriminating between right and wrong. William James in his fascinating textbook on psychology employed a striking illustration of the functions of the mind. He pictured the mind as a judge seated on his tribunal. Through the afferent nerves of the senses cases are brought to the judge for his decision. He weighs them carefully, rejecting the spurious ones and giving orders to the will to execute the worthy impulse. Thus the mind is the honest intellectual broker estimating the relative values of the many clamorous desires and impulses which are listed, as it were, on the psychological market, and recommending to us investment in the sound ones. In other words, complete honesty of mind, or intellectual piety, is the very foundation on which moral character is built. It is the *sine qua non* of ethical religion.

I am well aware that thus to attribute to mind the dominant role in the shaping of one's religion will seem to many little short of impiety. Ever since the beginnings of the Christian church the orthodox have regarded the free use of the intellect as inimical to faith. "Free-thinker" has become a term of reproach—as if anyone would wish to be a slave-thinker! The African church father Tertullian exclaimed, "What has Jerusalem [piety] to do with Athens [intellect]!" The medieval church historian Martin of Tours deliberately cultivated an ungrammatical style to show his contempt for learning. Martin Luther declared that his reason was the harlot of Satan. If a protest was made against the acceptance of unintelligible doctrines, it was met by rebuke or persecution. When the brilliant

Abelard of the University of Paris complained, "How can I teach what I don't understand?" his opponent St. Bernard thundered in reply, "Believe, don't reason!" But belief is not a matter of the will. A man can no more "will to believe," in spite of William James's valiant apologia, than he can pull himself up by his bootstraps. Belief inexorably follows on the weight of evidence; and the evidence is furnished by the mind. To maintain, therefore, that any subject is too sacred to be investigated by the human mind is to deny that the truth of it can be substantiated. Thus the opponents of the free exercise of the intellect in religion become the real "infidels," denying faith in the faculty of man which distinguishes him from the animal creation and raises him to a dignity which makes him the arbiter of true and false, right and wrong. That is the justification for the bold affirmation of the Scottish philosopher Sir William Hamilton: "In the world there is nothing great but man; in man there is nothing great but mind."

There are of course many mysteries which the intellect cannot grasp. We must be content to let them remain mysteries; for, as Goethe said, man was not made to explain the universe. However, there is a great difference between what transcends man's reason and what offends man's reason. John Locke pointed out this distinction some three centuries ago in his *Essay Concerning Human Understanding;* but the theologians have shown a willingness to ignore the distinction. They argue for a creed on the plausible ground that man, as a rational being, must seek

INTELLECTUAL PIETY

to give his religion a basis in a formulated and systematic body of belief. No one, I think, would deny the propriety and even the necessity of such a procedure. The scientist, the statesman, the physician, the educator, the lawyer all operate on such a plan. They have certain convictions concerning the aims and purposes of their professions, and they seek to relate their discoveries and test their experience against the body of tradition which they have inherited from the past. Why, then, is not the theologian's creed on just the same intellectual level as the physicist's hypothesis of the conservation of energy or the physician's hypothesis of fatal bacteria? The question seems fair; but the argument is spurious, because it overlooks some fundamental differences between a religious creed and a scientific hypothesis.

First of all, the creed deals with propositions which are not merely unverified but are unverifiable. It makes certain statements about the nature of God, the divinity of Christ, the three persons of the Trinity, the plan of salvation, the bodily resurrection of Jesus, and the last judgment, which are not only incapable of proof but also incomprehensible by the human mind. All the above clauses are taken from the Apostles' Creed, which is the basis for all the creeds and which is recited in all the orthodox churches. Examine the creeds of Christendom in Professor Philip Schaff's bulky volumes with that title, and you will find that they all contain these unverifiable assertions. If the modernist preacher no longer seeks to expound, explain or recommend to his congregation such doctrines as the Trinity or the descent of Jesus into hell, it still remains true that they are there in the creeds which most of the Christian churches preserve to this day. It is said that Benjamin Jowett of Balliol, when repeating the Apostles' Creed, was in the habit of inserting *sotto voce* the words "used to" between the "I" and the "believe." Would it not conduce to intellectual piety to abandon frankly the incomprehensible and unverifiable doctrines which make up what Santayana called "the epic of salvation," and so leave the churches, freed from the embarrassment of apologetics, to devote their energies to preaching the religion taught by Jesus and St. Francis and Ralph Waldo Emerson rather than to the theology taught by St. Augustine, Thomas Aquinas and John Calvin?

A second feature of the creed which distinguishes it from a scientific hypothesis is its claim to finality. There is nothing provisional or tentative about a creed. It professes to be ultimate, unamendable truth which no newly discovered facts of nature or newly attained insights of philosophy can change. How utterly different are the hypotheses of science, which, even held for long generations by the majority of men, are nevertheless open to modification and even to discernment in the light of new knowledge. Consider for how many centuries men believed that the earth was the center of creation and that the sun and moon revolved around it to give it light by day and night, with the planets circling about it, each in its crystalline sphere, and the stars above fixed in the vault of the sky—all as portrayed in the majestic *Divine Comedy* of Dante. Then came Copernicus and Kepler and Galileo to revolutionize this medieval conception, supplant astrology with astronomy and reveal the true relation of the earth to the heavenly bodies. The scientific mind, convinced by the testimony of the telescope and the mathematical tables, laid aside its false hypothesis of the geocentric universe; but the church, nurtured by a creed of finality, fought the new truth for generations. It forced Galileo to his knees and compelled him to recant. Martin Luther called Copernicus "a fool" who turned the world upside down and flew in the face of divine Scripture. Did not the Bible say that Joshua bade the sun to stand still in the valley of Gideon, and the Psalmist speak of the sun going forth like a bridegroom from his chamber? What more was needed, then, than the "word of God" to prove that it was the sun and not the earth that moved? The same story of ecclesiastical resistance in the name of a creed to newly discovered facts in other fields of science can be read in Andrew D. White's classic volumes on *The Warfare Between Theology and Science.*

A third important difference between a religious creed and a scientific hypothesis is the alleged divine sanction which attaches to the former. To question, probe and test a tradition of science or history is the privilege, nay, the bounden duty, of the scholar. It is obedience to the command of intellectual piety. It is by that method that every advance in knowledge has been made. And no scientist deserves the name who is not ready to abandon an hypothesis when its inadequacy to account for the facts is demonstrated. But to question or deny the assertions of a religious creed has ever been, and still is in the eyes of the orthodox, an act of rebellion and intellectual presumptuousness. "Heretic" and "infidel" are the opprobrious terms applied to the doubters, however honest and humble they may be. No stigma is attached to a man who, in the light of new knowledge, gives up the long-cherished theory of the solid and indivisible atom, or who is persuaded in his mind that a democratic regime is more conducive to the welfare of society than an autocracy. But if he finds himself unable to believe in the dogmas of the creed he is forthwith regarded as morally perverse. The very word "miscreant," which literally means a person with a wrong belief, has come to be synonymous with "wicked." And "heretic" should be a title of commendation rather than condemnation, since it means one who exercises his free choice. Theology was hailed through the Middle Ages as "the queen of the sciences." But those were the days before experimentation supplanted argumentation as the avenue to truth. The queen has been removed from her throne. The scholastics of the Middle Ages were as keen intellectually as any philosopher of today. But they spent their mental energies in the discussion of theological subtleties which have no relevance to our spiritual needs. For example, St. Thomas Aquinas, the greatest of them, and a man whose works are studied diligently in the Catholic seminaries today, devotes most of his voluminous *Summa* to the discussion of the nature of God, Christ, the Trinity, angels and demons, and only

INTELLECTUAL PIETY

at the end comes down to man. The Franciscan Roger Bacon characterized these fine spinners of theological arguments as "men tumbling about in their own conceits."

In no other field than religion has man been bound in conscience to theories formulated in ages of comparative ignorance. In no other field is there more despite for Tennyson's true words:

> *There is more faith in honest doubt,*
> *Believe me, than in half your creeds.*

And all this because the creeds have been surrounded by an aura of sanctity which has defended them against what Thomas Huxley called "a religion of common sense," that is, a religion of intellectual piety. The scholarly and refined Leo XIII has often been called the first modem pope; and we readily acknowledge the breadth of his views on social questions such as the labor problem. Yet on the dogmas of the creed he was adamant. Here are his words in the encyclical "Libertas Humana" (1888): "It is entirely unlawful to demand, defend or grant unconditional freedom of speech, of writing, or of worship." But what freedom can man enjoy if the greatest of all freedoms, the freedom of religion, is denied?

We do not despise tradition. It is only from the experience of the past that we can draw the wisdom to shape the course of the future, both in our individual lives and in the evolution of society. But it is as a guide and not as a jailer that we should take the past if it is to have instruction and inspiration for us. Loyalty to tradition and bondage to tradition are quite different things. It is the use and not the mere perpetuation of tradition which contributes to enlightenment and progress. The letter killeth; only the spirit giveth life. Conformity, which is the aim of the creed, is like an opiate in religion, dulling the spirit of adventurous search and lulling the mind into complacency. It was satirized by John Dryden in his allegorical poem "The Hind and the Panther":

The good old bishops took a simpler way;
Each asked but what he heard his father say,
Or how he was instructed in his youth,
And by tradition's force upheld the truth.

The vast expenditure of intellectual energy to bolster the creeds of Christendom stands convicted of futility by the testimony of history. From the days of the first heretic martyr down, the countless attempts of bishops and kings to compel uniformity of worship and belief have failed. The mightiest ruler of his day in Europe, the Emperor Charles V, waged war for thirty years to force his rebellious Protestant subjects to return to the Catholic faith. He abdicated in 1555 and retired to a monastery to end his days. There he busied himself with tinkering with clocks, and one day a truth dawned on his perverted mind. "How foolish of me," he said, "to expect to make men think alike when I cannot get two clocks to tick alike." The famous Spanish inquisitor Torquemada was a gentle and kindly man, we are told. Yet he was guilty of the torture and death of tens of thousands of his fellow men only for the crime of obeying their conscience. It is true, thank heaven, that the age of torture and slaughter to compel men to confess a faith which they did not hold has passed. But this happy progress is due to the humanizing influence of science, historical research, wider contacts in trade and commerce, the spread of education and many other secular factors slowly working to undermine the authority of religious dogmas. Sectarianism has made no contribution to this change in the intellectual climate. The creeds contain not a line in recognition of religious freedom. And if the clergy of today acclaim religious freedom, as they so generally do, they do so not in obedience to the creeds they are supposed to defend but in despite of them. Is it too much to hope that the day will come when the antiquated and incomprehensible creeds of Christendom, over which for centuries vain disputations have been waged and bitter persecutions inflicted, shall be relegated to their proper place as merely historical documents which, like their contemporary speculations in other fields, testify to the intellectual maturity (or immaturity) of the age in which they were produced?

Now, in this insistence on intellectual piety we do not ignore the fact that in the long process of evolution the intellect is a late-comer in the family of human faculties. In the infancy of both the race and the individual the emotional exhibitions of will and desire are primary. Even before he can walk or talk the infant is constantly reaching out for something, and the little child is forever saying, "I want." Desire is the spring and motive of all man's activities. It is coterminous with life itself. The writer of the book of Ecclesiastes was on sound psychological ground when he made the lack of desire synonymous with a lack of further interest in life. The time has come for the silver cord to be loosed and the golden bowl to be broken and the dust to return to dust. Note the words in which the Preacher describes the approach of this severance of earthly ties: "And desire shall fail." The writer of the Epistle to the Hebrews identifies faith with desire in his definition: "Faith is the substance of things hoped for." It is not the "just" alone who live by faith. All men do. The hard-boiled, aggressive businessman has faith in the satisfactions and prestige which the accumulation of a fortune will bring. The diligent scholar who scorns delights and lives laborious days has faith in the rewards of a mind stored with knowledge. The religious mystic has faith in the joy and peace which he anticipates in union with the divine will. Even the gangster and the criminal have faith, faith in the perverse doctrine that the temporary gains from their antisocial conduct outweigh the satisfaction to be got from earning an honest living. If it were not for the intervention of the mind to weigh and curb the manifold desires and impulses of men by subjecting them to that enthroned arbitrament of the intellect which William James described, the line between truth and falsehood, right and wrong, would be blurred or blotted out, and ethics would mean nothing more than custom. That is why we contend that intellectual piety is the measure of all pieties. "Mind is king," said the old

INTELLECTUAL PIETY

Greek philosophers, who were the first to free the mind from its bondage to the mythologies based on emotional figments. And mind is king not only in the secular fields of science and politics and philosophy, but also in religion. Even those who seek to dethrone the mind from its sovereignty here are obliged to employ the tools of the intellect in their arguments.

Not that emotions and desires have no place in ethical religion. They are the sources of inspiration. It is an uplifting emotion to sense with Kant the majesty of the starry heavens above us and the moral law within us. It is a noble desire that reaches out for the vision of perfection which has sustained the faith of the great prophets of righteousness through the ages. "The deepest thing in our nature," says William James in his *The Will to Believe,* "is this dumb region of the heart in which we dwell alone with our faiths and our fears. As through the cracks and crannies of caverns those waters exude from the earth's bosom which then form the fountain-heads of springs, so in these crepuscular depths of personality the sources of all our outer deeds and decisions take their rise." The sources, yes, but not the direction of the streams of conduct which flow from the sources. When Pascal wrote that the heart has reasons which the mind knows not of he misused the word *reasons.* The heart does not have reasons. It has emotions and desires: love, sympathy, aspiration on the good side, and, in our Dr. Jekyll and Mr. Hyde natures, hatred, callousness, cowardice on the evil side. It is the function of the intellect to furnish the reasons for our behavior by virtue of its power to discriminate between the emotions and desires which should be cherished and those which should be vanquished. That is why we affirm that intellectual piety is the prime factor in ethical living.

Note, please, that it is intellectual integrity and not intellectual attainment on which we are insisting. We make no pretense to superior knowledge. We are as cognizant as any mystic of the vast amount of truth which lies outside the present range of human knowledge and which may forever lie outside it. Nor do we agree with Matthew Arnold that man has all the knowledge needed for right living, but only lacks the will to put his knowledge into practice. There are ever new insights to dawn on the mind, but the only way to build them into character is to remain strictly faithful to such insights as we already have. Integrity is a qualitative and not a quantitative word. And it means honesty in religion as well as in business or science or sport. The man who resorts to sharp practices in business is condemned because he is undermining the very foundations on which alone honest business can be built. Likewise, those who resort to sharp practices in religion, such as the preaching of doctrines in which they no longer believe, or performing ceremonies which no longer conduce to spiritual growth, or the evasion of the patent meaning of a passage in Scripture by giving it an allegorical interpretation, are undermining real religious faith. The whole subject of apologetics, which is part of the curriculum in theological schools, is only a refined version of the casuistry which Protestants have so often condemned in Catholic theology. And there is a peculiar temptation for a priest or minister to subordinate strict intellectual integrity to an emotional appeal, because, unlike men in other professions, he is pledged by ordination vows to the support of doctrines which he may find difficult, as his mind matures, to reconcile with his convictions. Intellectual piety forbids us to give hostages to any system or theory, however hallowed by tradition or fortified in institutions, which stands in the way of the attainment of new knowledge and new insights. In a purely ethical religion, such as we advocate, there can be no conflict between intellect and faith, because no advance in knowledge, no enlargement of the understanding, no refinement of critical acumen can impair the majesty of the ethical ideal.

A noted political scientist wrote that democracy must be interpreted anew by every generation. That means that with the ceaseless activity of man's mind and the consequent welter of political and economic theories, each generation finds itself living in its own peculiar social atmosphere, or "climate of opinion," as Professor Whitehead has called it. Obviously, the Jeffersonian democracy of a small agrarian country, with an abundance of land for the nurture of a sturdy yeomanry, its antipathy to the concentration of population in urban centers (those sores on the body of the country), its jealousy of any infringement of the federal government on the rights of the states, its dread of a strong executive and a nonelective Supreme Court, presents a great contrast to our present conception of a democracy which must adapt itself to a huge industrial country, with its problems of conflicting class and sectional interests, its demand for the planned integration of its chaotic economic activities, and its need of a strong and wise guidance in the new responsibilities forced upon it for its contribution to the peace of the world. The *ideals* of democracy have not changed since Jefferson's day. His plea for evenhanded justice, incorruptible public faith, freedom of speech, press and religion in his first inaugural address is reiterated a century and a half later by the chief magistrate of the nation. The ideal remains like an inextinguishable beacon to illume the path of the statesman; but the path itself must lead through perplexities and obstacles which only a faithful adherence to intellectual integrity can master.

Do we not see need for the application of new experimental means to reach desired ends in every field of human enterprise? The ideal of the law is justice; but what tremendous changes are taking place in our generation in the conception of the way to secure justice, with the substitution of conciliation boards, arbitral tribunals, family relation and juvenile courts for the formal and final pronouncements of judge and jury governed by inflexible legal precedents. The ideal of education is the elicitation of the mental and moral potentialities of the student; but what a revolution has taken place in the last generation in the methods calculated to realize this ideal.

So it is with religion. The ideal is the attainment of spiritual stature., This, I think, no adherent of any sect or creed would deny. But what a change we are witnessing today in the conception of the way to attain spiritual stature. How the emphasis on orthodox dogmas is fading out among the more broad-minded theologians and preachers, giving way to a humanistic approach. I read the other day the address of a prominent New York minister to the graduating class of a theological seminary. The title of the address was "The Truth of the Gospel," and the one question that superseded all others, the speaker said, was, Are the central affirmations of the Christian faith realistically true? But through the entire address the speaker made no reference at all to the "central affirmations of the Christian faith," which are the fall of man in Adam, his redemption through the vicarious sacrifice of Christ, the bodily resurrection of Jesus from the grave, his ascent into heaven to resume his seat at the right hand of God, and his coming again to judge the world, when sinners shall be consigned to the flames of hell and the saved rewarded with eternal life in heaven. The young men were not bidden to go into their pulpits to preach these doctrines, as they would have been bidden in our grandfathers' time. Instead they were told of "the reality of the moral order that inflexibly brings to men and nations the harvest of what they sow," that "every falling bomb and rumbling tank, every starving child and heartbroken home are preaching Christianity [!] today," that "the present world calls for a new confidence in presenting Jesus' *ethical* teaching." This is a far cry from "the central affirmations of the Christian faith." The address was an exhortation to preach ethical religion. And many a liberal minister today is preaching sermons, whatever concessions to traditional forms may be made in the ceremonial part of the service, that would be appropriate to the platform of an Ethical Society.

On January 31, 1945, John D. Rockefeller, Jr., delivered an address at a dinner given by the Protestant Council of the City of New York on the future of the Christian church. "To establish spiritual righteousness in the world," he said, "to build up an internal rather than an external religion, to emphasize the responsibility of the individual to his Maker, was Christ's mission on earth. . . . What the world craves today is a more spiritual and less formal religion. To the man or woman facing death, great conflict, the big problems of human life, the forms of religion are of minor concern, while the spirit of religion is a desperately needed source of inspiration, comfort and strength. . . . [This] natural craving for religious guidance must not be repelled by alphabetical lists of denominal churches and agencies, when what they seek is so fundamental, and sectarian differences are so superficial." For this courageous subordination of confessional orthodoxy to ethical demands Mr. Rockefeller was promptly taken to task by Bishops Manning and De Wolfe. But I am sure that the vast majority of people were on Mr. Rockefeller's side. The proof is that no sensible man would ask whether a person to whom he would entrust his family or his money was a Presbyterian or an Episcopalian, but only whether he was an honest man. In view of this dawning recognition of the primacy of ethics over creeds, it is incumbent on us of the Ethical Societies to present to a confused age, in which the "winds of doctrine" are carrying the pollen of religious doubts and despairs far and wide, as clear and simple a statement of the elements of our faith as we can. I shall attempt to do this in the following chapter.

CHAPTER SIX

THE ELEMENTS OF ETHICAL RELIGION

THE EARLY Christian fathers were in the habit of enumerating the *Notae,* as they called them, or the distinguishing marks of the true faith. The winds of doctrine blew where they listed in those formative days of the church, carrying the pollen of heresy here and there. In a little village of Phiygia in Asia Minor a prophet by the name of Montanus appeared claiming that the Holy Ghost had spoken to him directly with a special revelation. Did not the Scripture say that the Holy Spirit would descend on the disciples when Christ had gone and guide them into all truth? Had it not come on the day of Pentecost and inspired them to "speak with tongues"? Why should it not continue to select its chosen instruments where it would? Were the days of prophecy ended? There were also many gospels, visions, epistles, revelations circulating among the churches, claiming to be "Scripture" and containing a veritable hodgepodge of doctrines with long and, except to theologians, forgotten names, like Monophysitism, Docetism, Patripassianism, over which men fought gladiators in the arena. Read Kingsley's novel *Hypatia* and you will get a vivid picture of those fierce doctrinal battles.

Now obviously, the church, if it was to build up a great authoritative institution as the sole depository of the true faith, could not allow these diversities of doctrine to go unchecked. If anyone outside the consecrated ranks could lay claim to as authentic a revelation as that contained in the Gospels and the Pauline Epistles, where would the revelations end? The polls must be closed to further prophecy, and the pretenders must be branded as false prophets. If the validity of the sacraments were made to depend on the moral character of the priest who administered them (as the Donatists asserted), they would be robbed of their inherent magical force. If a man could by his own efforts make any step toward salvation (as the

Pelagians asserted), the unmerited grace of God would be thwarted. So the fathers wrote heavy tomes against the heretics, emphasizing over and over again the true "notes" of the church, and building up through four centuries that imposing structure of dogmatic hierarchal authority which culminated in the vast pretension of the bishop of Rome to be the vicar of God on earth and the head of the church outside of which there was no salvation. *"Extra ecclesiam nulla salus*

In this chapter we are asking what are the *notae* or distinguishing marks of ethical religion as contrasted with the crystallized dogmas of theological religion. One may ask, Are not these marks clear? Have we not for three-quarters of a century been proclaiming them from our ethical platforms? Should they not be well known by now? They certainly should; but the mere mention of the words "Ethical Culture" to those outside our fellowship shows how little comprehension they have of what we stand for. What do you believe? is the question put to us again and again. How do you differ from the churches and the synagogues? Felix Adler once told of an experience which he had while crossing the ocean on the same ship with a high dignitary of the Catholic Church. In their friendly conversation the prelate asked him what the Ethical Society stood for. When Dr. Adler explained that it was a creedless religion which taught the supremacy of ethics over dogma, the prelate said to him, "But surely you believe in the fundamental doctrines of the virgin birth and the incarnation." He had been living for years

THE ELEMENTS OF ETHICAL RELIGION

in New York, with the opportunity of reading week by week the discourses of Dr. Adler. He was supposed to keep up with the religious thought of his contemporaries, as well as to be versed in the traditions of his own faith. Yet he could not grasp the meaning of a purely ethical religion or imagine a religious teacher for whom such "fundamental doctrines" as the virgin birth and the incarnation were a matter of indifference. If such was the reaction of an educated man high in the office of the church, it is little wonder that the so-called man in the street has no clear idea of the meaning of ethical religion.

But aside from the haziness of public opinion on this subject, there is another reason why we should attempt to set forth the distinguishing marks of our ethical religion. That is to show that it has the right to the name of "religion." The Department of Commerce of the United States does not deign to include the members of Ethical Societies in its statistics of religious bodies. Likewise the armed forces refuse to allow a registrant to specify "Ethical Culture" as his religious affiliation on its blanks, requiring him to sign as Catholic, Protestant or Jew. Whether this discrimination is due to the fact that we are so few in numbers as to be negligible or to the view that we are a group of rebels against religion, it is accepted even by many who, with a rather chilling politeness, regard us as well meaning people who do not know what religion really is. At one of our anniversary meetings a noted minister spoke on our New York platform. He paid tribute to the

ETHICS AS A RELIGION

fine character of Felix Adler and praised the work the Society had done in its educational, charitable and civic activities. A few weeks later this minister declared from his pulpit that Felix Adler preached a "religion" from which the very heart of religion was left out—meaning of course the Christian "epic" of man's fall and his redemption by the death of Christ. But so to narrow the definition of religion is sheer provincialism. Can anyone who is acquainted with the spiritual history of man deny that noble religions existed centuries before Christianity came into the world, or that, in the present anguished state of society, men are reaching out for a new definition of religion which shall satisfy both their intellectual integrity and their moral aspirations? May it not be that we are even now entering a post-Christian rather than an anti-Christian era? If so, it does not mean that religion has been banished from men's hearts. For the quest for a satisfying religion cannot be driven from the heart of man by the supersession of any of the forms in which religion has expressed itself in the past.

As the forehead of man grows broader so do his creeds,
And his gods they are shaped in his image and answer his
   needs.
And he clothes them with thunder and beauty, and he
   clothes them with music and fire;
Seeing not, as he bows at their altars, that he worships his
   own desire.

THE ELEMENTS OF ETHICAL RELIGION

One more point I must make before proceeding to an analysis of the elements of ethical religion. In our fellowship no one speaks with the authority of a priest or minister representing a venerable institution or proclaiming the truth of a divine revelation. We are seekers together for light on the way of our pilgrimage, each striving to bring to the common task such insights as have been vouchsafed to him, and each eager to profit spiritually by the religious experience of his fellow seekers. It is with this intent that I ask you, in the phrase of Woodrow Wilson, "to lay your thought alongside of mine," in this discussion of the elements of ethical religion. "Come now, and let us reason together" is the Biblical text which appeals to me as the most fitting for a fellowship of seekers.

First and foremost is the conviction that the ethical end is supreme over all other ends in life. That is our absolute categorical imperative. It does not proceed from the demand of any extraneous power or the authority of any established institution. We do not hold with Matthew Arnold that it is "a power not ourselves that makes for righteousness," but rather that no righteousness can exist except by the power within ourselves. The doctrine of an "imputed" righteousness which figures in the creeds is a contradiction in terms. For if righteousness is imputed, the efforts of the individual to attain it are nullified. This is the flaw in the whole system of vicariousness, whether it be that of the suffering of a divine victim for our sins or that of the attribution of our capacity for virtue to a "power without ourselves." The sins may be many and the virtues few; but such as they are, they are our own. And therein lies the stem responsibility of each of us for the ceaseless attempt to eliminate the former and increase the latter. No man can serve two masters or two master ideals. One or the other must be supreme. And by asserting that ethics is the supreme ideal we mean that every religious doctrine, rite, custom and tradition must be brought to the bar of ethics to justify its acceptance. This does not imply that there is no inspiration for us in the faith that in our striving for ethical perfection we are in harmony with a universe in which physical order is based on moral law. Indeed, such faith in the supreme ethical nature of reality seems to me a necessary postulate for the conviction of the ethical imperative in our individual lives. Some call it doing the will of God, others getting in tune with the infinite, others helping to build the golden city. It makes little difference in what terms this sense of copartnership is expressed. The important thing is that it is there, an inescapable datum in human consciousness. There may be a greater or less admixture of mysticism in it, for that depends on the distinctive psychological bent of the individual. There may be a firm belief in the existence of God, or a reverent agnosticism which is content with the indubitable truth that if God does not exist no assertion of man can create him, and if he does exist no denial of man can destroy him. We do not, then, seek to banish mystery or exclude theism in our declaration that ethics is the supreme end of man. We only insist that all varieties of religious expression and opinion be brought to the touchstone of ethical judgment to test their validity. Are they directly translatable into ethical conduct? Do they actually promote right living? If not, they are nothing more than empty formalities or idle speculations.

This affirmation of the supremacy of the ethical end is in sharp contrast to the place assigned to ethics in the creedal religions. They teach ethics, to be sure, but they do not teach the supremacy of ethics. It is an ethics qualified by an adjective. For example, the phrase "Christian ethics" is constantly used as if it were synonymous with ethics itself. The implication is that ethics is a corollary of the Christian faith, whereas ethics is prior to Christianity both in time and in logic. To make Christianity the source of ethics is to confuse the cause with the effect, or, in common parlance, to put the cart before the horse. We might as well speak of a Christian astronomy or a Christian mathematics—which reminds me that a few years ago the president of a Baptist college in the South wrote to Columbia asking the university to recommend to him a professor of Christian biology. That Christianity, like all the higher religions, is deeply concerned with ethics is true; but that it is the matrix of ethics is the reverse of the facts.

A second major element in ethical religion is the affirmation of the infinite worth of every human being. This too is a doctrine approved by Judaism and Christianity. But the grounds on which they base their affirmation are different from ours. In Judaism the doctrine is characterized by the introduction of a racial element: namely, the idea of a "chosen people," the seed of Abraham. And in the Christian theology a man's worth is not intrinsic, but is conferred on him by the grace of God. Man was created in God's image; but he lost the resemblance through Adam's sin of disobedience, and thenceforth all the descendants of Adam became *unworthy* wretches, whose alleged virtues were, in St. Augustine's words, only "shining vices" *(splendida vitia)*, and whose cloak of righteousness only "filthy rags." No hard-boiled cynical politician, no scorner of the "damned human race" like Frederick the Great, no "sawdust Caesar" like Hitler or Mussolini could take a meaner view of human nature than that set forth in the creeds of Christendom. To what extent the acceptance of their doctrine of man's corruption can lead is nowhere more dismally shown than in the case of the New England minister Jonathan Edwards. Edwards has been celebrated by recent biographers as the keenest intellect in the America of the eighteenth century. He was a devoted husband and father. Yet the duty which he felt incumbent upon him to defend the harsh theology of John Calvin transformed him into the zealous misanthrope who preached sermons on such texts as "The Eternity of Hell Tortures," "The Torments of the Wicked in Hell No Occasion of Grief to the Saints in Heaven" (even "saved" wives would not bemoan the punishment of their "lost" husbands), and "Sinners in the Hands of an Angry God." He terrified his congregation by comparing them to spiders hanging over the bottomless pit of fire by a slender thread which might break at any moment. He called them "vipers, hissing and spitting poison at God." Even infants and little children, for no other crime than that of having been born with the curse of Adam upon them, were numbered among the vipers. And this man thought he was a Christian! Did he perhaps misread the words of Jesus as "Suffer the little vipers to come unto me, for of such is the kingdom of heaven"? What a calamity that brilliant intellectual gifts should have been devoted to the merciless logic of the theologian. Let the biographers bestow all the praise they will on the genius of Jonathan Edwards; the fact remains that he was an ethical pervert.

Now, the ascription of infinite worth to every human being is a piece of folly in the eyes of those who point to the wastrel and the criminal. How can you call the drunkard or the murderer a person of worth? they ask. They are confounding a man's worth with his value to society. His value may be nil. He may even be a curse to society. Yet we affirm his worth. Why do we do this? In the first place, because he is a member of the *corpus spirituale,* the great spiritual community of humanity. We must still, however great his failings, attribute to him worth, because only so can we be assured of our own membership in the spiritual community. If there were a celestial potter who by his own arbitrary will fashioned one vessel to honor and another to dishonor (as St. Paul so unethically declared), then we might flatter ourselves, as the old Puritans did, that we belonged to the honorable pottery. But we can lay no such flattering unction to our soul. We are part of a common humanity, and the possibility of worth in any must be predicated on the possibility of worth in all. Value is measurable; but worth is unmeasurable. There are no scales of value in such things as love, honor, fidelity, integrity and sympathy. They cannot be computed. For worth is qualitative, not quantitative.

A third element in ethical religion is the method which we advocate for proving the infinite worth of the human being. The Golden Rule reads: "Whatsoever ye would that men should do unto you, do ye also unto them." Confucius stated it in the negative form: "What you would not have men do unto you, do not to them." Neither statement puts the emphasis on the attempt to kindle in another a desire to do the right for its own sake. It is too much like a bargain. You treat me well and I'll treat you well. Again, the famous Kantian maxim, "So act that your conduct might be taken as the universal norm," lacks the humility which should characterize the ethical ideal. Who am I, with all my faults and failings, to set up my conduct as the standard to which others should conform? Even the best of men knows in his heart that some baser alloy of selfishness, jealousy or pride is mixed with the gold of his intentions. No individual can serve as a paragon to be copied by others. The ethical rule or maxim, so often repeated from our platform, is "Act so as to elicit the best in others and thereby in thyself." The emphasis is on the word "elicit." It is a precept of mutual stimulation. It recognizes the need for reciprocity in the cultivation of the ethical life, which is the meaning of our phrase "Ethical *Culture."* We attribute worth to the individual, then, because it is only to the worth in him that we can make the ethical appeal, and from worth in him that we can receive the reciprocal stimulus to our own ethical endeavor. And we call this worth infinite because there is no limit to the process of exchange. By himself a man is an insignificant creature. It is only in his give-and-take relations with his fellow men that he can attain moral growth. "A talent may ripen in solitude," wrote the poet Goethe; "a character only in the stream of the world."

What a relief, then, it is when we change the emphasis from belief to conduct. We are freed from the —haunting sense of guilt which has caused agony to so many people who have not been able to accept the doctrines which they have been told to believe on pain of eternal punishment. We are delivered from the fear of unbelief, which is the great tragedy of religious history. To the overanxious efforts of the theologians to explain the nature and will of God, there succeeds a tranquillity of mind which is content to leave the mystery of human existence to the realm of mystery, where it must forever belong. Man must learn, as a wise philosopher put it, "to sleep on the pillow of doubt." But not only does ethical religion liberate us from the lingering feeling of obligation to subscribe to doctrines which more often hinder than help our efforts to attain spiritual stature, but it also furnishes us with the strongest motives for pursuing that task. It is stimulating as well as liberating. It appeals to the hidden springs of potential virtue in man, bidding him to clear them of the silt of selfishness and the dried leaves and sticks of indolence, so that their waters may well up in life-giving freshness. "Conversion" is a word commonly used for the profession of a change of heart under some emotional strain. It is even applied to the mere formality of substituting one form of worship for another, as when, for example, a princess brought up in the Greek Orthodox faith is "converted" to Romanism in order to marry a Catholic prince—the conversion consisting in the hurried recital of a catechism and the profession of new vows. But religion cannot be put on and off like a garment. It is the lifelong task of converting the moral imperfections of one's character into incipient virtues. To take a simple illustration, it is like the process of making steel. From the crude iron ore the impurities like carbon and sulphur must first be removed, and then to make the finer grades other elements, like chromium, tungsten and molybdenum, must be added. So do we have to eliminate from our religion the impurities: the superstitions which have come down from a primitive age, the uncharitableness which has characterized sectarian rivalry, the equivocations which have been so often resorted to for the justification of dubious doctrines. Then, to this negative duty we have to add the precious elements of courage and patience and love which are needed for the finer product. Can anything be more stimulating than this challenge to the literal conversion of the crude ore of the empirical self into the shining product of our aspirations? As James Cotton Morrison has truly said, "A passionate ideal of excellence can so fill the mind that no pleasure is felt in anything but the effort to realize it."

Professor Arthur M. Schlesinger, Jr., in his remarkable book *The Vital Center* castigates the "doughface" liberals who have opposed weasel words to the hard realities of fascism and Communism, and calls for a revival of the pragmatic radicalism which has characterized the best periods of American history. It may be that some critics of the elements of ethical religion treated in this chapter will find them also liable to the charge of wishful platitude. Why not face the obvious fact that man is a poor weak vessel md treat him "as such, instead of insisting on the fiction that he is an induplicable personality of infinite worth? But is it a fiction? Is not the sternest reality in life just the experience which comes to us when in our best moments we are "in tune with the infinite," when with Wordsworth we feel

> *A presence that disturbs us with a joy*
> *Of elevated thoughts, a sense sublime*
> *Of something far more deeply interfused,*
> *Whose dwelling is the light of setting suns.*
> *And the round ocean and the living air,*
> *And the blue sky, and in the mind of Man.*

"Glory to man in the highest, for man is the master of things," wrote Swinburne. But man's glory is not in the mastery of things; it is in the aspiration of his soul. At times we are tempted by the all too obvious failure of men to claim their birthright of spiritual worth to let our faith in their capacity flag. In a momentary lapse from his customary robust faith in humanity, Walt Whitman expressed his disgust with the cowardly supineness of his fellow men:

> *I think I could turn and live with the animals . . .*
> *They do not sweat and whine about their conditions;*
> *They do not lie awake in the dark and weep for their*
>   *sins;*
> *They do not make one sick discussing their duty to*
>   *God.*
> *Not one is dissatisfied; not one is demented with the*
>   *mania of owning things;*
> *Not one kneels to another, nor to his kind that*
>   *lived a thousand years ago;*
> *Not one is respectable or industrious over the whole*
>   *earth.*

We may dismiss this outburst of admiration for the placidity of the animals as a momentary irritation with his fellows' "failure of nerve." We may be sure that the author of "Pioneers, O Pioneers" would not be content to turn and live with the animals. The good gray poet would share his life with his fellow men, for all their dissatisfactions, weeping, and kneeling, rather than with the old gray mare. And he amply atoned for his despite of man's "doughface" religion by his lines in the poem "Starting From Paumanok":

THE ELEMENTS OF ETHICAL RELIGION

*I say the whole earth and all the stars in the sky are
   for religion's sake.
I say no man has ever yet been half devout enough,
None has ever yet adored or worship'd half enough,
None has begun to think how divine he himself is,
   and how certain the future is.
I say that the real and permanent grandeur of these
   States must be their religion. . . .*

"The most powerful thing in the world," wrote Victor Hugo, "is an idea whose time has come." Quietly, persistently, inexorably that idea ripens into actuality like the fruit which matures in the vernal sun. The time for the emergence of a forward-looking, democratic, universal religion of ethics is at hand. The world is waiting for the sunrise of a common faith which shall inspire its new-found and travail-born resolve to gather the nations into a common fold of humanity. How near or how distant the daybreak of that faith may be we do not know. But the signs of its dawning are multiplying every year that passes. The footprints of history are pointing toward that goal. The future is with ethical religion.

CHAPTER SEVEN

AN ETHICAL CONCEPT OF GOD

One of the questions inevitably asked of a member of an Ethical Society is, Do you believe in God? At first sight this seems like a simple question which can be answered by Yes or No. But in reality it is a very complex question. Everybody except the avowed atheists (and they are comparatively few) believes in some kind

AN ETHICAL CONCEPT OF GOD

of God. Even the devils, we are told, "believe and tremble." And no tribe of men has ever been found that did not have its gods. The proper question to ask, therefore, is not the futile one, Do you believe in God? but rather, What *kind* of God do you believe in? Leaving to the anthropologists the study of the kinds of gods that enlisted the beliefs of primitive peoples, let us, by way of clarification, distinguish the different kinds of God believed in by our contemporaries.

First, there are the theists, who believe in a personal God: that is, in a God with whom they can communicate in praise and prayer and who communicates to them his will and purposes in revelation. He cares for them as a father cares for his children. His providence guides them through all the way that they must travel. They say with Newman,

> *Keep Thou my feet, I do not ask to see*
> *The distant scene; one step enough for me.*

All Christians are theists; but not all theists are Christians. No man ever had a more vivid sense of God's guidance than Mahatma Gandhi; yet Gandhi did not abandon his Hindu religion for Christianity. Abraham Lincoln gave ample evidence of his belief in God's providence; but he never made profession of the Christian religion. Countless other examples of ancient and modem believers in a God who presides over the destinies of men should warn us against the bigotry of Calvin's assertion that Christianity was the one true religion and all the others "a vast welter of error." The name "theist" is derived from the Greek (*theos*) word for God. The Latin for God (*deus*) furnishes us with another type of believer—the deists.

For the deists God was no less real than for the theists. But he was not a personal God. He was the creator of heaven and earth, and, having seen that his work was "good," he left it to pursue its appointed course. Man was not an object of his continual care. Nature furnished sufficient evidence of his benevolence, and the "natural religion" of the deists meant living in accord with the harmony of nature. Though ancient philosophers like Plato and the Stoics taught the doctrine of man as an aspirant for the perfection of God and a spark of the divine, it was in the eighteenth century that deism developed into an important type of religion. Most of the fathers of our republic were deists: Jefferson, Madison, the Adamses, Paine, among others. They did not believe in the inspiration of the Bible or in miracles or in the orthodox plan of salvation. For them Jesus was not the second person of the Trinity, but a revered teacher of the good life on earth. They regarded a man's theological opinions as a matter of private interest, not to be forced on others by church or state. Thomas Jefferson was the most articulate of this group of men. He was accused by his orthodox critics of being a "French atheist"; but in fact his attitude toward religion was deeply reverent. He made a synopsis of the Gospels. In his magnificent Statute of Virginia for Religious Liberty (for which he asked

AN ETHICAL CONCEPT OF GOD

to be remembered, along with the Declaration of Independence and the founding of the University of Virginia) he wrote: "Well aware that the opinions and beliefs of men depend not on their own will, but follow involuntarily the evidence proposed to their minds; that Almighty God hath created the mind free, and manifested his supreme will that free it shall remain, by making it altogether insusceptible of restraint; that all attempts to influence it by temporal punishments or burthens, or by civil incapacities tend only to beget habits of hypocrisy and meanness . . . that to compel a man to furnish contributions of money for the propagation of opinions which he disbelieves and abhors is sinful and tyrannical; that our civil rights have no dependence on our religious opinions any more than on our opinions in physics or geometry . . . and finally, that truth is great and will prevail if left to itself, errors ceasing to be dangerous when it is permitted freely to contradict them: We, the General Assembly of Virginia do enact that no man shall be compelled to frequent or support any religious worship, place or ministry whatsoever, nor shall be enforced, restrained, molested or burthened in his body or goods, or shall otherwise suffer on account of his religious opinions or beliefs; but that all men shall be free to profess and by argument to maintain their opinions in matters of religion, and that the same shall in no wise diminish, enlarge or affect their civil capacities." In his later life he showed considerable interest in the Unitarian movement, which was growing in New England, and three years before his death he wrote to a friend: "I am a Christian in the only sense in which Jesus wished anyone to be; sincerely attached to his doctrines in preference to all others; ascribing to him every human excellence, and believing he never claimed any other."

The professed atheist is a person who does not believe in the existence of God. The term has always been one of reproach, implying moral corruption. But this is manifestly unfair and invidious. An atheist may be a man of exemplary character. He is simply one to whom the evidence for the existence of God presented to his mind is unconvincing. The agnostic, often confused with the atheist, neither affirms nor denies the existence of God. He dismisses the question as one beyond the scope of the human mind and regards all attempts to prove or disprove the existence of God as a waste of effort which should be spent in the study and the improvement of man himself. "How can I understand God," said Confucius, "when I do not know men?" I pass by other conceptions of God or gods, such as pantheism, polytheism and dualism, as of little or no significance for modem man.

Having thus noted some of the current conceptions of God, we may proceed to the subject of the chapter: an ethical concept of God. And I say *an,* not *the,* for the latter article would imply that the Ethical Societies had an "official" doctrine of God. That is not so. Each leader and member of such a Society is left perfectly free to entertain whatever opinion of God appeals to his mind or his emotions. I am therefore presenting my own ethical

AN ETHICAL CONCEPT OF GOD

concept of God, without knowing whether or to what extent my colleagues and associates would agree with me; and I am submitting it to the reader for whatever judgment he thinks it merits.

In the first chapter of Genesis we read: "God created man in his own image, in the image of God created he him." What can such a phrase as the "image of God" mean to us? Surely, man was not created with the attributes commonly ascribed to God of omniscience, omnipotence and omnipresence. And what worthy image of God have men ever had except the projection into infinity of their own highest ideals: justice, mercy, love? It is these ideals that we worship. We may be awed by infinite power, but we cannot really worship it, because it is not a worshipful (worthful) ideal. Therefore, I believe, it would be truer history and better psychology to read the text: "Man created God in his own image, in the image of man created he him." If this seems to some like a brash and impious assertion, the whole course of human history is there to prove that the idea of God has grown in worthiness *pari passu* with the growth of man in knowledge, integrity and charity. Many a religion has perished because its authorized guardians clung to a concept of God, or gods, whose character failed to measure up to the progress of man in ethical insight; for, as T. S. Eliot has said, "No religion can survive the judgment of history unless the best minds have collaborated in its construction."

My concept of God is based on the argument of the

preceding paragraph. It is not concerned with the existence or nonexistence of God; for, as we have noted, that question is beyond human determination. Near the close of the eighteenth century Immanuel Kant of Konigsberg published a book entitled *A Critique of Pure Reason,* which is acknowledged to be the keenest analysis of the powers of the human mind ever written. He demonstrated that, since the mind operates only within the limits of time and space, it can never grasp transcendent truths. But Kant, inheriting from his mother a strain of pietism, was not satisfied with this negative conclusion. Like Pascal, he believed that the heart has reasons which the mind knows not. Hence he wrote another work, *A Critique of Practical Reason,* in which he set forth three "postulates" (demands) which must be assumed in order to satisfy a man's religious cravings: namely, the existence of God, immortality and a future state of reward and punishment. We would agree with Kant in his analysis of the limited power of "pure reason"; but not on the necessity of assuming his three postulates as a guarantee of a life of religious devotion. No one would deny that Buddha was a deeply religious man, and that Buddhism, before it was degraded into a system of priestly idolatry, was a noble religion. Yet Buddhism had no God. Nor is a belief in immortality a necessary postulate for a religious life. It would be impossible to say with how many people vague "intimations" of immortality crystallize into positive belief; but it is certain that unnumbered multitudes of religious people subscribe to the motto, "If there

AN ETHICAL CONCEPT OF GOD

be no other life, pitch this one high." And as for future rewards and punishments, the truly religious man needs no bribes or threats to keep him in the path of virtue. I am not arguing against Kant's postulates. They may, for all we know, be true. But they are not indispensable for the religious life.

If, then, we are not satisfied with the theistic conception of a God who personally directs the life of every individual and has prepared an endless life of bliss or torture beyond the grave; or with the deistic conception of a God who, on the contrary, having created man, has no concern for his conduct or destiny; or with the atheistic denial of any kind of God at all; what can we offer as an ethical concept of God? Some of our members are opposed to the use of the word "God." But we must have some term to denote the aim and fruition of our ethical aspirations; and it seems to me that there can be no objection to the use of the word "God," if we bear in mind that it is the *kind* of God we mean.

Now, for a person for whom ethics is itself a religion, and not merely an adjunct to religion as in the current idea of the church, any concept of God must be a purely ethical one. Omniscience, omnipotence and all such incomprehensible attributes of God are excluded, not because they are disproved, but because they are not ethical. The picture of a great Being enthroned in heaven, surrounded by angels and saints "casting down their golden crowns" before him, is a childish one. I remember in my tender years thinking of God as a bookkeeper with pen in hand, setting down my youthful sins to confront me at the Day of Judgment. If in the minds of the more mature similar concepts of God have lost their vividness, is it not true that for most people the idea of an enthroned God who directs all the vicissitudes of their lives is a vague and hazy one? The Westminster Shorter Catechism declares that the chief end of man is "to glorify God and enjoy him forever." But neither of these phrases corresponds to the working life of men. Man can add no "glory" to a Being by hypothesis the sum of glory himself; and enjoying God forever is an idea which seems to have little relevance to the tasks that man has to grapple with on earth. The father image of God, which Jesus emphasized, is much more practical and comforting than the king image which finds so general an expression in the liturgy and hymns of the churches. But when we consider the persistent strife of men and nations, can we truthfully say that the conception that all men are brothers because they are sons of a common father has availed to inspire them with the sense of brotherhood? Another doubt as to the sufficiency of the theistic conception of God arises from the fact that it is difficult to see the intervention of Providence in the vicissitudes of life. The walls of a certain church in Paris are covered with plaques thanking God or a saint for the cure of a disease or deliverance from some danger or even success in passing an examination. One is reminded of the story of the man who visited a Roman temple hung with such votive

AN ETHICAL CONCEPT OF GOD

tablets and asked, "Where are the tablets of those who perished?"

Acknowledging the vast superiority of the theistic concept of God over the deistic or the pantheistic, I would still reverently maintain that there is an ethical concept in better agreement both with human experience and with human aspirations. Instead of positing a personal God, whose existence man can neither prove nor disprove, the ethical concept is founded on human experience. It is anthropocentric, not theocentric. Religion, for all the various definitions that have been given of it, must surely mean the devotion of man to the highest ideal that he can conceive. And that ideal is a community of spirits in which the latent moral potentialities of men shall have been elicited by their reciprocal endeavors to cultivate the best in their fellow men. What ultimate reality is we do not know; but we have the faith that it expresses itself in the human world as the power which inspires in men moral purpose. We have not yet begun to exploit men's ethical potentialities. Too much occupied with what is called their relations with God, we have neglected the more fruitful study of their relations with one another. I like the reply of Thoreau when someone asked him in his closing hours if he had made his peace with God: "I am not aware that I ever quarreled with him." The concept of God (or, better, Godhead) which posits as ultimate reality a spiritual society is not, as some of our reverend critics have charged, a subtle form of ego-theism. We claim to be members of such a society not because we have *attained* spiritual stature, but because we are intent on attaining it. Our concept of the spiritual society as the pattern to which human society should conform is the ever urgent impetus which bids us to persist in our efforts to purge the baser elements out of our lives and realize our birthright as members of the *Corpus Spiritual*. "The true Shekinah, the glory of God, is man," wrote St. Chiysostom.

Religion has been almost exclusively concerned in the past with the problem of man's relation to God. The more practical problem of man's relation to his fellow man has been slighted. But more and more we are realizing that the individualistic conception of salvation which was the chief concern of our grandfathers is no guarantee of a spiritual society. "The trouble with this town," remarked a friend of mine of a community in which there was a good deal of religious smugness along with social bickerings and backbitings, "is that most of the people have been 'saved.' " In the final volume of his remarkable Lanny Budd series, *O Shepherd, Speak!,* Upton Sinclair writes: "Emphasize, enrich and build up by discovery the side of man concerned with his spiritual powers, his potentialities that still remain to be fully explored, and we get into things that command respect and interest, sympathy and fraternal feelings. Why not then put everything we have behind the search for these transcendent powers of the mind, these spiritual relationships which man is capable of having with other men, transcending distance and lan-

AN ETHICAL CONCEPT OF GOD

guage and color and national boundaries?" This is genuine ethical religion. It is worthy of our utmost devotion. It is being increasingly endorsed by philosophers (see John Dewey's *Our Common Faith)* and psychologists, who discover what marvelous potentialities for spiritual vision and growth there are in man. And it is faith in these potentialities, however feebly we see them exemplified in our current society, that warrants us in attributing indefeasible worth to every human being. As no two faces are exactly alike among the millions we see, so no two souls are alike. Each is induplicable, distinctive, indispensable in the ethical concept of a Godhead of ultimate moral power.

I know that a great majority of people would deny the name "religion" to the concept of God which has been offered in these pages. They feel the need of a personalized symbol—a father or savior or pope or saint—whom they can adore. "I cannot give up my faith," was the reply of a woman to my attempt to state the position of the Ethical Societies, as if devotion to ideals and the building of a community of interrelated seekers for spiritual perfection were not worthy to be called a "faith," but no more than a hobby, like golf or the collection of stamps! We do not need, in pursuing the envisioned goal of ethical religion, to carry with us our old gods, like Aeneas leaving Troy for the new lands "promised by fate." In the beatitudes of Jesus there is no mention of dogma or ceremony. The blessings are for the pure in heart, the merciful, the peacemakers, and those who hunger and thirst after righteousness—all *ethical* qualities.

We agree completely with the accumulating pleas of clergy and laymen for a revival of religion as the only remedy for the unspeakable moral degradation of this hate-filled, war-shattered age. Monday morning's newspaper devotes several columns to the report of sermons delivered the day before; and the burden of the sermons is a conventional exhortation to honor and obey God. What do such expressions as "loving God" or "obeying God" actually mean in our daily life? One cannot love infinite power and majesty. One can love only the qualities of goodness which one finds in one's fellow men, and one can obey only the dictates of one's own conscience. All else is the product not of love but of fear. "If a man say, I love God, and hateth his brother, he is a liar," wrote the author of the first Epistle of John; "for he that loveth not his brother whom he hath seen, how can he love God, whom he hath not seen?" Thus the "God" that we love is not the figure on the great white throne, but the perfect pattern, envisioned by faith, of humanity as it should be, purged of the evil elements which retard its progress toward "the knowledge, love and practice of the right."

Is this ethical concept of a God (or Godhead) less real, less inspiring, less reasonable than the orthodox concept of an absolute creator and ruler of the universe? Is it not even more consistent with man's actual experience than the theistic concept of a God who determines all the vicissitudes of one's life and numbers the hairs of one's head? Does it not offer to the large number of men and women for whom the Jewish and Christian articles of belief and forms of worship no longer have significance, a faith to satisfy their intellect, enlist their enthusiasm, and beget in them a renewed sense of their dignity and responsibility as contributors to the building of the "golden city" of light?

CHAPTER EIGHT

IS ETHICS ENOUGH?

THE ACID TEST of any religion is its effectiveness in pervading the total thought and action of men: in the home, in business and the professions, in politics, in education, art and science. Does ethical religion meet this test? Does it furnish us with inspiration to face the vicissitudes of life with courage and confidence? Does it strengthen our resolve to reach ever higher levels of purpose and conduct? Does it enable us to preserve a spirit of equanimity and fortitude when frustrations and bereavements come? Is it a sustaining faith? I spoke in an earlier chapter of a distinguished New York clergyman who took part in the celebration of one of the anniversaries of the Ethical Society, and warmly congratulated the Society on its contribution to the civic improvement of the community in its educational and charitable work; and who, a few weeks later, declared from his pulpit that Felix Adler had a religion from which the very heart of religion was left out—meaning, of course, the doctrine of salvation through faith in the atonement of Christ for the sins of men. Ethics, in his opinion (and in the opinion of churchmen generally), was indispensable. It was good enough so far as it went, but it did not go far enough. Unsupported and unsanctioned by belief in a supernatural revelation, it was only a vain attempt of man to lift himself up by his own bootstraps, an attempt bound to end in impotence and pride. If this is true, it is a fatal indictment of ethical religion. Are we deceiving ourselves? Are we attempting to play *Hamlet* with Hamlet left out? Are we feeding on husks, while the fatted calf is waiting for us in our father's house? Are we being content with a second-rate or a third-rate religion? Are we hitching our wagon to a will-o'-the-wisp instead of to a star? These are questions which go to the very root of our ethical faith. Here is the challenge we must meet.

ETHICS AS A RELIGION

I need not pause to take up the charge brought by fundamentalists and evangelical revivalists that men deliberately spurn the salvation offered by Christ because they want to continue a life of sin. That is not only a base slander against many of the noblest characters the world has ever seen, but it is also a silly misunderstanding of the motives which determine human choice. For no sane man would exchange the chance of an eternity of bliss in heaven for a few brief years of riotous living on earth if such a choice appeared to him as a real alternative. A Faust, wearied by years of closeted study, might yield to the tempting's of Mephistopheles and sell his soul to the devil in return for worldly indulgence. But no Spinoza or Emerson or Lincoln was ever impelled by such a motive to reject a theological creed which seemed to *him* an intellectual stultification or a moral equivocation. "Let us eat, drink and be merry, for tomorrow we die" has ever been the philosophy of fools. We may, then, leave these fundamentalist critics of ethical religion as deliberate rebellion against God to their own satisfaction in thinking of themselves as the chosen instruments of God for warning men to flee from the wrath to come. Our concern is with another sort of critic, who commends our ethical earnestness and regards us not as stiff-necked rebels against religion but rather as mistaken people who have tried to make a religion without using the necessary ingredient of religion: namely, belief in a divine revelation contained in the Bible or communicated by the church.

IS ETHICS ENOUGH?

Now, in spite of the fact that we have a great number of religious sects in our country (over two hundred varieties of Protestantism), there are at bottom only two kinds of religion: one which accepts a supernatural revelation and the other which finds in man himself the capacity for autonomous spiritual development. Between these two conceptions of religion there is a great gulf, unbridgeable by argument, because there is no common ground for argument. The difference between Catholicism and Protestantism is trivial, for example, as compared with the difference between supernatural and nonsupernatural religion. For while the Protestant Reformation did away with many things, such as papal authority, pilgrimages, purgatory, Mariolatry and the veneration of the saints, what it kept was of far more significance than what it rejected: namely, the whole scheme of salvation as formulated by the fathers of the church. We of the ethical faith adhere to that type of religion which finds in man himself the capacity for autonomous spiritual development. We believe that the appeal to such capacity has been the theme of all the great religious prophets of history, including the greatest of them all, Jesus of Nazareth. The sufficiency of this faith is denied by the upholders of a supernatural revelation. How can you have a faith, they say, without the sanction of a supernatural power to whom you pay worship? Let me emphasize the word "sanction" in this objection. It is not a question of the *existence* of such a power. That is a matter beyond the scope of the human mind; though I think few would deny the existence of a power transcending our comprehension. The question is whether there can be a vital religion which finds its sanction in human experience and relationships, regardless of the existence or nonexistence of a Deity beyond the skies. I quote from a recent sermon of a Methodist minister before a conference of some seven hundred religious educators, deploring the fact that religion has been "pigeonholed" and God has been "denied the responsibility for the salvation of mankind" . . . that the task of a Christian is "to contribute to what God is trying to do in building his kingdom on earth." What sense can such a phrase as "what God is trying to do" make to a mind not obfuscated by theological verbiage? And what an utter confusion of thought it is to assert in one breath that man is depriving God of "the responsibility for the salvation of mankind" and in the next breath to call on man to help God in "what he is trying to do"!

But the futility of argument between those who believe that at a given time and place a final truth was revealed from heaven to be set down in a sacred scripture and guarded by a sacred institution, and those who believe that religion has come out of the progressive refinement of man's moral sense, is obvious. There is no common ground from which to start. The dilemma is illustrated by a card which was displayed in the subway trains a few years ago, advertising the screen play of Franz Werfel's popular novel *The Song of Bernadette.* There we read the comment of the Dean of Lourdes on the miracle of the apparition of the Virgin to the simple French maid:

IS ETHICS ENOUGH?

"For those who believe in God," said the Dean, "no explanation is necessary; for those who do not, no explanation will suffice." In other words, belief in God means the acceptance of an hallucination as a fact, and the refusal of such acceptance means disbelief in God. Now there are millions of devout souls who cannot for a moment so deny the light of reason as to believe in a kind of God who chooses to manifest his power by miraculous signs and wonders. Ethical religion has no place for such a God. It does not descend to the level of thaumaturgy.

In asking whether ethics satisfies our religious needs, we must realize that, since we are individualized personalities with wide differences in tastes and temperaments, our religious needs will be expressed in various ways. A person with a highly developed aesthetic nature will crave artistic elements like music and colored windows, while a more puritanical nature will find such accessories of religion rather a hindrance to his concentration upon moral duty. In religion, as in every other phase of life, a man's peculiar bent or set of nature comes out. Charles Darwin, for example, was wholly without aesthetic appreciation. Music, as he confessed, was to him only noise. He never read poetry. Biological science satisfied his spiritual need. Another great scientist, Albert Einstein, finds release for his emotions in playing the violin. Given these varieties of temperament, can we discover one supreme need of man to which all others are subordinate and on which they all focus? I believe that we can, and that this supreme need is the need to attain such harmony of desire and duty as shall bring him inward peace and joy. There are many paths to such harmony of life. Some approach it along the way of mystic meditation; others through intellectual enlightenment; others by devotion to social reform; and still others by the acceptance of the authority of a religious tradition weighted with the prestige of age and numbers. A Thomas a Kempis, a Socrates, a Jane Addams, a Cardinal Newman, stand as examples of these various approaches. We do not deny the value of any of these paths to inward harmony and peace. What we deny is the denial that a purely ethical religion can furnish such a path.

One of the indictments brought against ethical religion is that it is not a religion at all, but a rejection of religion. We are looked upon by many as a group of dissidents interested mainly in asserting what we do not believe. Our attitude is represented as a Mephistophelian one: *"der Geist der stets verneint."* This misunderstanding is perhaps due to the motto we have used at times, "Deed, not Creed." The two terms are not meant to be mutually exclusive, but to indicate the relative importance of each. Deed comes before creed, because it is conduct which testifies to the soundness of belief. We fully agree with Carlyle's dictum that a man's faith does not consist in the things which he does not believe. We have as positive a faith as that of any orthodox sect. And if that faith makes invalid for us various articles of traditional belief, that is no more than every new religious interpretation of the past has done for the traditional faith of its time. The birth of Christianity, the Protestant Reformation, the rise of religious toleration, the acceptance of the modem scientific and critical spirit by all except the fundamentalists is proof of the withering of old blossoms when a new bud is put forth. Many years ago a noted minister preached a sermon on "The Expulsive Power of a New Affection." There is the same expulsive power in every new religious insight and experience. It makes a belief or practice which once seemed important now no longer significant. Thus Emerson left the pulpit because praying in public and the celebration of the Lord's Supper ceased to be a source of nourishment for his religious life. He did not attack or ridicule the traditional rites of the church; he simply found them an encumbrance instead of an inspiration.

The truth is that every affirmation carries with it a denial of some sort. They are the obverse and the reverse of the same medal. If we affirm our belief in liberty, we condemn slavery in the same breath. If we affirm the absolute supremacy of ethics, we thereby relegate other aspects of religion, like creed and ceremony, to a subordinate place. The negations are incidental to the affirmations. A simple example may serve as an illustration of this point. If a man wishes to promote a real estate development in a hitherto unpopulated area all he has to do is to plant his stakes and run his projected streets according to his blueprints. But if the district is populated a certain amount of demolition will be necessary to clear the way for the new development. The demolition is not the objective, but the reconstruction. So has it been with every advance in human knowledge and every social reform. Ptolemy yields to Copernicus; Aristotle to Bacon; Nostradamus to Newton. So it has been and must be in religion. It is the innovators and not the traditionalists who have ever renewed and repristinated the religious life of the world. And their appeal has always been to the latent ethical potentialities in man. Witness the Buddha, Asoka, Marcus Aurelius, Gandhi—and Jesus of Nazareth.

History furnishes us with the reason for the persistent denial by the orthodox of the sufficiency of ethical religion. All the great religions of the world originated in Asia. It was a land of absolutism. Great God-descended monarchs ruled their slave subjects with a rod of iron and led mighty armies to conquer their neighbors. They sat on jeweled thrones, demanding obeisance and adulation. Men came crawling to their feet with the salutation "O King, live forever!" Power was the essence of their life. And the gods conceived by these peoples were gods of power, absolute, arbitrary, raised far above the human mass. Even the Jehovah of the Hebrews was originally a terrifying thunder god dwelling on Mount Sinai. As man became more humane so did his gods. The awful thunderer Jehovah, leader of the hosts of Israel in battle, became the ethical god of the prophets, his power undiminished, but exerted for the triumph of righteousness. And with Jesus he became the loving father of all mankind. Nevertheless, traces of Asiatic origin continued to

IS ETHICS ENOUGH?

exist, and still do exist, in religion. The God of Calvin was an oriental monarch, wrapped in majesty and power, requiring obeisance and adulation. And do we not see in the hymns sung in the churches today (with perhaps little realization of the significance of the words) the influence of this Asiatic idea of enthroned pomp and military prowess: "Oh worship the King, all-glorious above," "Crown him with many crowns," "The Son of God goes forth to war," "Come, thou almighty King," and many more of like tenor. The complement of this exaltation of the might of God has been the depreciation of man. In spite of the Psalmist's declaration, "Thou hast made him a little lower than the angels, and has crowned him with glory and honor," orthodox Christianity has been savage in its denunciation of man as a corrupt being from birth, ruined by the fall of Adam. The Vicar of Hoddeston emptied his church of its more respectable members by beginning his sermons with the words "Fellow worms."

It is against these twin doctrines of an arbitrary God and corrupt man that we protest. They have been responsible for the persecutions, barbarities and hypocrisies which have stained the pages of religious history. We set in opposition to them the doctrine of the dignity of man. We are as keenly aware as any evangelist of the shortcomings of ourselves and our fellows; but we assert that the way to overcome these evils is through the constant effort to obey the divine voice of duty within ourselves, each act of obedience helping us to hear that voice more clearly and to heed it more faithfully. We need no command from on high. The command is in our hearts. The hope of heaven is no incentive and the fear of hell is no compulsion to the fulfillment of that inward command:

> *Virtue could see to do what virtue would*
> *By her own radiant light, though sun and moon*
> *Were in the flat sea sunk.*

It is held by the supernaturalists that without the promise of rewards for virtue and the threat of punishment for sins, in a future existence, the vast majority of people would lose the sense of moral obligation and society would, in Tennyson's phrase, "reel back into the beast." This is a sad confession that, in their view, man is incapable of devotion to a good life from the purely human motive of *noblesse oblige*. They will admit that a few exceptionally fine natures may not need bribes or threats to keep them in the path of righteousness, but contend that for the ordinary run-of-the-mill people such supernatural sanctions are necessary. This is a direct result of the low estimate of human nature which is taught by the creeds. If our religious leaders were as diligent in encouraging men in the cultivation of their ethical potentialities as they have been in persuading them of their incapacity to lead a righteous life, they would be astonished at the response they would meet with. For people by and large do want to live up to their best levels, and are eager to have their ethical duties clarified and their ethical resolves stimulated.

IS ETHICS ENOUGH?

The doctrine of evolution was the most fruitful discovery of the nineteenth century. It has colored all our thinking and revolutionized our science. Its great protagonist, Charles Darwin, confined the doctrine strictly to biological phenomena. By Herbert Spencer, Youmans, Fiske and others it was extended into the social field to explain the development of institutions. But the most momentous step in human evolution has never been explained. No one has been able to detect the stage in man's development at which conscience, the sense of right and wrong, and the duty to follow the right and shun the wrong, entered into his mind. Yet that was the critical moment of human evolution. Then began all that is of worth in our world: truth, justice, love. Then man came into his birthright as a being "crowned with glory and honor." Then religion was born, the religion of ethics. And whenever a sick age has risen in new strength to throw off the accumulated poisons of injustice, lethargy, superstition or despair, it has been by virtue of a rebaptism of ethical fervor; whenever a sick soul has recovered peace of mind and zest for life, it has been because a new ethical stimulus has roused him to a realization of his privilege to be a member, even the humblest member, of the company of those who, undaunted by adversity or despite, have carried forward the banner of truth.

This ethical approach to religion has a liberating effect. There is a fine passage in the little volume entitled *On the Religious Frontier* by Percival Chubb, for many years leader of the St. Louis Ethical Society.

ETHICS AS A RELIGION

"It is with a blessed sense of relief from anxiety as to belief [writes Mr. Chubb] when the axis of the mind is changed from belief to conduct. A man should know that his responsibility for his beliefs hinges upon his responsibility for the conduct of his life. He cannot put beliefs off and on as he does his clothes. . . . Let religion then cast away this vestige of its ancient fear and fret lest one should miss some preordained way of thinking about the universe, life, God; and a burden is lifted from the mind. It is free. It accepts. It does its best. It does not cling fearfully to suspected beliefs as if suspended over a precipice of destruction. This then is the emancipation that comes with the removal of belief and creed from the first plane in one's religion to the second. Living comes first, and living is a progressive undertaking. We must not cease to grow, because growth is the sign of life. So our beliefs will grow and change. There can be no finality, no fixation."

When we think of the immense amount of suffering which good people have undergone because of the fear of misbelief instilled into them by the doctrines taught them in early years, we can appreciate what a relief it would be to young and old alike if the whole sanctified scheme of salvation and all the magic paraphernalia handled by the priesthood were laid on the shelf, and our religious leaders devoted their energies to the task of helping men to discover and fulfill their duties to their fellow men. Let no one think that their congregations would be less satisfied or less edified by such a leadership. The people do not want or need dogmas; they want guidance in the conduct of life. They know that they fail often and wander from the path of righteousness; but they are neither so naive as to attribute their faults to corruption inherited from the fall of Adam nor so cowardly as to expect an innocent proxy to atone for those faults. In John Bunyan's famous allegory when the Pilgrim Christian reaches the beautiful gate, the burden of sin which he has carried on his back rolls off and he rejoices as a free man. For centuries men have carried on their backs another burden, the burden of irrational, incomprehensible and persecution-provoking creeds. May we not hope that, as they come to the beautiful gate which opens on the avenue of the ethical approach to religion, this burden too will roll off their backs and leave them free to work out their salvation, not "in fear and trembling," but in courageous effort for the disciplining of their own souls and the redemption of society.

Do you say that this is vain optimism, utopianism, wishful thinking? Well, the very fact that men have envisaged the possibility of gaining the mastery over the evil traits in their own nature and over those destructive forces of hatred and war which threaten the life of our civilization is proof that it is not a vain chimera. And what is stirring in the nations today but a crusade for a utopia: that is, for a world order such as has never been before? And as for wishful thinking, what other kind of thinking is worthy of an ethical being? We have had plenty of despairing, pessimistic thinking which has been pleased to call itself "realistic." Its champions, the Nietzsches and Spenglers and the like, have played the part of a Machiavelli or a Mephistopheles, exploiting the baser traits of human nature as the foundation for their philosophies, and assuming an air of pitying condescension for the foolish idealist. But has the world been better for their insistent judgment that it could hardly be worse? Have they furnished cheer and courage to their fellow men to wage the battle against evil? Have they given guidance along the road that leads man to the attainment of his true moral stature? No, it is the idealists who are the genuine realists, because the real person is the person for whom ideals are the breath of life.

On the great seal of the United States is the motto *Novus Ordo Seculorum,* a New World Order. Such was the prophecy of the founders of our little republic of less than four million souls, who, in the words of James Madison, "reared the fabric of a government which had no model on the face of the globe, and which it was incumbent on their successors to improve and perpetuate." It was indeed a "new order," a government founded on the consent of the governed and dedicated to the proposition that all men are created equal; a government which subordinated the military to the civil power, recognized no feudal obligations or hereditary classes, and guaranteed to every individual the precious rights of the freedom of speech, of the press, of worship, of assembly and petition. In recent years the motto of the great seal has been

IS ETHICS ENOUGH?

on everybody's lips. The Nazis bragged of their purpose to establish a new world order which should last a thousand years. The Japanese announced a new world order which should bring eastern Asia and the islands of the Pacific into their so-called "co-prosperity sphere." Mussolini boasted of restoring the Roman dominion of the Caesars. And today the democracies as well as the aggressor nations are convinced that the world is facing such revolutionary changes in political precedents, economic practices, educational theories, and the estimates of national interests and international responsibilities as to create a veritable new order. We in America believe that we shall cling to our fundamental democratic institutions, though they will inevitably be modified by large increases in governmental power. We believe that our traditional faith in the value of private initiative and beckoning opportunity will survive, though many of the selfish and unsocial practices which have characterized our economic system in the past will have to be eliminated. We believe that the American ideal of a great peace-loving nation, founded on the principle of justice and dedicated to the mission of fostering liberty at home and abroad, will not be lost, although a present emergency compels us to resort to weapons which we would fain have banished from the earth. It is not given us to see just what sort of new order will eventually emerge from this greatest upheaval in the history of mankind. But that it will be so unprecedented as to make the nineteenth century look like the Middle Ages few can doubt. The millions of mankind the world over are, in the late Mr. Willkie's phrase, "on the march." Just where to they do not know, but they sense that it is into a new order that they are moving. The final judgment of history on Adolf Hitler may well be that he was a chosen instrument of destiny, not to usher in a thousand years of slavery for all men except the German race, but to awaken a complacent and apathetic world to a fresh realization of the blessings of human liberty.

In the new order to which we look forward with mingled hope and trepidation no trend of thought or action can be exempt from the searching examination which the crisis of a great transformation brings. It is not alone our political traditions that we must bring to the bar of world judgment, nor our economic system that we must readjust to meet the awakened demand for a better justice, nor our international prejudices and rivalries that we must seek to sink in a real community of world fellowship. We must also search our hearts with utter frankness to inquire whether we as individuals are cultivating the moral qualities which are the basis for all the reforms, political, economic, educational, social, which the new order demands. In other words, we must bring religion into the picture. For, although the deliberations of the statesmen and the plans of the generals are concerned with political and military problems, and the reports of the conferences at Casablanca, Moscow, Cairo, Teheran, and Potsdam have little or nothing to say of religion, it is nevertheless true that the ultimate directive in shaping the mind of the makers of policy is a religious conviction. We should not have fought the war unless we believed that there was something supremely worth fighting for; and we should not have the idea of a supreme worth unless it were for a religious conviction.

A generation ago the democracies gained a complete victory in arms. The great idealist of that day, Woodrow Wilson, declared that it was the culminating victory in the struggle for liberty; and when the armistice was signed he went before Congress to announce that everything that we had fought for had been won. But he was sadly mistaken. The fruits of victory turned into the ashes of defeat, as national selfishness, pride and rivalry sabotaged the peace. Now we have a second chance, and perhaps a last chance, to create the new world order. Can we believe that, with the lesson of the past two decades for our warning, the United States and the allied United Nations will throw away this chance? Dare we conceive that they will invite another orgy of material destruction and human slaughter by refusing to stand together for the defense of freedom? Shall we again be misled by such slogans as "Back to normalcy" or "America first" or "No foreign commitments" into repudiating the responsibility that goes with power and failing to follow up our great contribution to the winning of the war by the equally needed counsel for the preservation of the peace? Our answer to these vital questions will determine the success or failure of the new order. Religion must make its indispensable contribution. The spiritual life of the nation must be oriented toward sanity, sympathy and simplicity.

ETHICS AS A RELIGION

The vestiges of mummery must be eliminated from our worship and the survivals of sophistry and superstition banished from our creeds. We must raise a religious standard to which "the wise and honest may repair" without need to compromise their intelligence or camouflage their convictions. The time is ripe and overripe for a new religion to match the new order in secular things. The present crisis emphasizes the opportunity for the encouragement of a noble ethical religion, divorced from any slavish bond to tradition and based on manifest present human needs. We want no religious Gestapo and no evangelical demagogues. As the old sanctions fall more and more into disregard and disrepute, they must be replaced by a renewed faith in man's power to shape a destiny worthy of his endowment of reason and conscience. The new world order demands a religion of ethics.

CHAPTER NINE

A RELIGION FOR ADULTS

WHAT a marvelous charm there is in little children! How unreasonable they are, and yet how easily entreated; how egotistical, yet how abandonedly generous; how volatile, passing rapidly from laughter to tears and from tears to laughter. They are absorbed in the moment's desires, fears, hopes and disappointments. A piece of candy denied or a picnic postponed on account of rain means a ruined life. They live in a land of fairies and fables. They are our contemporary animists, endowing their dolls and Teddy bears with human attributes. They will have *Pinocchio* and *Babar the Elephant* read to them over and over again; and Santa Claus has a heavy mail at Christmas. How adorable they are, and how we hate to see them lose their childhood fancies with their milk teeth. But it is the law of nature. If, like Peter Pan, they never grew up, there would be no more children to delight another generation. So they pass on to adolescence and adulthood, and lay aside childish things. The fairies lose their wings and wands; Santa sheds his frosty beard; the fables are exchanged for the Elsie books and Henty, and these for Scott and Dickens, and these again for Shakespeare, Wordsworth, Emerson and Santayana.

But the gradations of adulthood are infinite. The human body is entirely renewed every seven years; yet a person of middle age is often recognizable in his photograph as a child. So it is with our mental and spiritual adulthood. The mature habits of thought and behavior are curiously mixed with childish elements. What could be more puerile, for example, than the behavior of a political convention, with all the ballyhoo of cheers and boos, of whistles, rattles, catcalls and paraded banners? How immature is much of our boasted educational method, with adherence to rote and repetition, its lack of perspective, its failure to bring the student into close acquaintance with the great creative geniuses in art, science, literature and statesmanship. When Thoreau was told that all the branches of learning were taught at Harvard, he replied, "And none of the roots."

Probably in no field of human interest is the duty of putting away childish things on reaching man's estate more conspicuously evaded than in the field of our deepest concern—religion. And the chief reason for the persistence of so many immature elements and childish conceptions in religion is, I think, that in their early impressionable years children have been taught to believe certain inexplicable propositions about God and the Bible, which not only did not correspond to the elementary capacity of the child but were invested with a sacred authority which made denial or doubt of them by the more fully developed intellect of the youth and the adult seem like rebellion and impiety. Orthodox religions have known full well how to use the plastic nature of the child's mind to inculcate professions of belief before the emotions have been sufficiently tempered by judgment to make them genuine beliefs. Catch them young, has been the motto. "Train up the child in the way he should go, and when he is old he will not depart from it." The ceremony of confirmation (the very word implying fixity and finality) is performed at a tender emotional age, when the recipient has impressed on him a faith which is really no "faith" at all because it is not a product of his experience. Then comes inevitable mental growth and with it often the agony of adjusting religious professions to actual convictions, which distresses so many adolescent minds, and results in making mere conformists out of the less resistant and cynical materialists out of the more resistant natures. In either case it is a loss to genuine religion and a spiritual calamity for the individual.

Much emphasis is placed on the comforts of religion; and I would be the last person to question the inward peace, the spiritual strength, the encouragement to better living which a real religious faith brings. But there is another aspect of religion which cannot be ignored, and that is the discomfort which the supposed necessity of believing in certain traditional doctrines has caused. When we think of the struggles that have gone on in the minds of young people outgrowing the religious teachings of their childhood, of orthodox parents who have grieved over the departure of their sons and daughters from the faith, or the wives who have agonized for the salvation of their husbands; when we think of the long series of wars waged to compel men to accept this or that dogma on the nature of Christ, the form of baptism or the authority of the pope; when we think of the unnatural, inhumane and cruel doctrines which men even of kindly nature, like a Torquemada, have felt obliged to support for the glory of God, it is evident that religion has been a bane as well as a blessing, a curse as well as a comfort.

Let me cite extracts from two religious poems. The first is from the New England puritan Michael Wigglesworth's "Day of Doom," a description of the last judgment. At their proper cue a swarm of infants appear before the awful judge on his throne, who addresses them thus:

A RELIGION FOR ADULTS

You sinners are and such a share as sinners may expect.
Such you shall have, for I do save none but mine own elect.
. . . Therefore in bliss you may not hope to dwell,
But unto you I shall allow the easiest space in hell.

With this kind concession the infants were dismissed to their doom, and doubtless they were the same infants with subsequent accumulations whom Jonathan Edwards a century or so later saw in his jaundiced vision crawling about the floor of hell. The other verses are from John Greenleaf Whittier's "The Eternal Goodness":

But still my human hands are weak to hold your iron
  creeds;
Against the word ye bid me speak the heart within me
  pleads.
I walk with bare hushed feet the ground ye tread with
  boldness shod;
I dare not fix with mete and bound the power and love of
  God.

The religion of Michael Wigglesworth and that of John Greenleaf Whittier present, like their poetry, a sharp contrast. The one is bombastic, conceited and inhuman; the other is humble, modest and sympathetic. One is puerile, for all its pretended omniscience; the other is mature in its honest simplicity. Wigglesworth was one of God's elect, who would doubtless have consigned the Quaker poet to a far less "easy space in hell" than that reserved for the infants. Whittier was a reverent agnostic with a heart of gold. Wigglesworth made religion nauseating; Whittier made it comforting. The late Lord Tweedsmuir (John Buchan) in his fascinating autobiography, *Pilgrim's Way,* tells how one of his dour Scotch relatives told him in childhood that Sir Walter Scott, "having neglected certain evangelical matters, was no doubt in torment." "The news," says Tweedsmuir, "gave me much satisfaction," for "the prospect of such company removed from me any fear of the infernal regions."

Now, obviously a religion for adults must recognize the qualities of the adult mind, among which are judgment, perspective, free inquiry, testing by experience, discrimination of values. Unassimilable doctrines, however hallowed by time, cannot be entertained. They create a mental indigestion comparable to the physical indigestion caused by unassimilable food. And no amount of apologetic pepsin, so freely administered by the theologians, can make them spiritually nourishing. A sound mind in a sound body is the test of adulthood, as contrasted with the vagaries of childhood, such as the ambition of ten-year-old boys to be fire engine drivers and twelve-year-old girls to shine before the footlights. Maturity means the harmony of desire, will and reason. We grow to be more and more a consistent whole, a personality. As Emerson says, "We cannot enter the temple of the cosmos disturbed in mind."

There is a place, an indispensable place, for religion in this ensemble of character. Only it must not be the religion of inexperienced, credulous childhood. I do not believe for a moment that when Jesus said, "Except ye become as little children ye cannot enter the kingdom of heaven," he meant to arrest mental development at infantile levels. He was rebuking his own disciples for their infantile squabbling as to who should be the greatest in the coming kingdom; and he told them that unless they humbled themselves they would not enter the kingdom at all. It was not maturing that he was condemning, but pride, conceit and selfishness, which are the negation of maturity. And to use the text to sanction mental irresponsibility as a synonym for holiness is a strange perversion of Jesus' meaning. Victor Hugo once spoke of a person who was "stupid to the point of sanctity."

There need not be any conflict between mature thought and religion in any field, and there never would have been such a conflict if men of the past, speaking in the name of religion, had not gone beyond the proper province of religion to announce theories of astronomy, cosmology, history, geology and the like, which the advance of science made untenable for the mature mind. There need not be any clash between religion and reason; and there never would have been such a clash had not the ethical teachings of Jesus been overlaid with dogmas borrowed from current metaphysics and oriental cults, and had not men converted religion, which is an aspiration of the heart, into theology, which Huxley said reminded him of quack medicine. There need be no warfare between religion and the state, and there would have been no such religious warfare as has drenched Europe in blood in past centuries, if ecclesiastical potentates and popes had not identified religion with the attainment of political ambitions and claimed, as representatives of God on earth, the right to depose princes and excommunicate peoples who did not submit to their dictation. They made religion synonymous with church and hierarchy, deriving therefrom the doctrine of the divine right of the church to control the political life of the people, as the Puritans did in seventeenth-century New England and the Jesuits tried to do in the reign of Queen Elizabeth. We in America have fortunately realized Cavour's ideal of "a free church in a free state"; but the poison of the centuries-old infection of religion by politics still lingers in many parts of Europe. And it provokes the counterirritant of the intrusion of politics into religion, as witness the official atheism of the Soviet regime and the Wotan-Valhalla religion of the Nazis.

It is not difficult to see the immature elements in these perversions of religion: the childish demand to have an explanation of mysteries; the ready acceptance of fanciful answers to perplexing questions, especially if these answers have a colorful appeal to the emotions; the eagerness to have one's own will (or willfulness) prevail as truth. Francis Bacon summed up the case against these assumptions and presumptions of immaturity in the words: "Those who take few factors into consideration arrive at decisions quickly."

We who plead for a mature religion, compatible with science and reason, are often represented as iconoclasts interested in the destruction of religion. But this is a complete misrepresentation. If the childish and irrational elements in religion disappear, it is not so much because we "reject" them as because they become irrelevant. They have come to have an historic interest rather than a compelling authority. One does not reject Santa Claus; one simply outgrows him. The benevolence for which he was a symbol is not lost when it is transferred to one's parents. I recall the amusing remark of a friend's five-year-old grandson who was beginning to have his doubts about Santa. "Well," he said, "if there isn't any Santa Claus it will cost daddy a pretty penny." Here was a transitional state of mind, a dawning sense of reality mixed with a lingering faith in a fable. Or consider another infantile belief, one entertained in fairly modem times by adults: namely, witchcraft. How widely this belief was prevalent two or three centuries ago can be seen from the exhaustive work on the subject by Professor Kittredge of Harvard. The saintly John Wesley declared that to disbelieve in witchcraft meant to reject Holy Scripture and deny Christianity. For did not the book of Exodus say, "Thou shalt not suffer a witch to live?" And how could a witch be put to death if witches did not exist? So we have the horrible episode in the late seventeenth century of the witchcraft mania in Salem, Massachusetts, when a score or so of poor mumbling toothless women were put to death as accomplices of Satan, largely on the testimony of frightened children and at the instigation of magistrates and ministers, a few of whom, like old Samuel Sewall, had the courage later to confess that they had been guilty of yielding to popular hysteria. Witchcraft,

ETHICS AS A RELIGION

like other infantile beliefs, was never disproved. It was simply outgrown. You cannot disprove a myth. John Wesley's logic is still sound, granting the premises. The command of the book of Exodus still stands. But no preacher today would use it as a text for a sermon.

One cannot study the history of the slow development of the adulthood of the mind without seeing how persistent has been the resistance of organized and institutionalized religion to practically every new discovery of science or fresh insight of reason. Innovation has always been branded as impiety. But there never would have been any kind of progress in the world had it not been for the innovators. Socrates was a great innovator. He taught the sons to aspire to know more than their fathers. He sought to replace the complacent worship of Apollo by an earnest search for the moral foundations of belief. Athens, he said, was a lazy stall-fed horse, and he was the gadfly sent to sting it into mental activity. For this inestimable service to his city, and to the world, he was condemned to drink the hemlock. Jesus was a great innovator. He offended the rabbis and the priests by his excoriation of the vain ceremonialism of current Judaism: the tithing of mint and cummin, the washing of the outside of the cup, the prayers offered in public places. He predicted the fall of the temple and violated the holy Sabbath. He gave his disciples "new commandments" and summoned them to a "better righteousness" than that of the scribes and Pharisees. And for these impieties he was sentenced to death by the Jewish defenders of the faith and allowed to be crucified by the Roman authorities. If the religion of his fathers had been "good enough" for Jesus of Nazareth there never would have been any Christianity.

Does all this mean that in gradually eliminating the immature and irrational elements from religion we lose the sense of reverence which is the very basis of religion? By no means! No scientist in his laboratory, no philosopher in his closet can ever discover a fact or build a system that will destroy the aspirations of the human heart. No sect or confession can have a monopoly on those aspirations. When we behold a glorious sunset or look on the transcendent majesty of mountain or sea, when we contemplate Immanuel Kant's dual source of reverence in the starry heavens and the moral law, we experience an indefinable elation like Wordsworth's "something more deeply interfused" in our limited grasp of things. Mystery there is. All we can do is to kneel before it. To attempt to explain it only robs it of its majesty and makes us babblers. Poetry ceases to be poetry when it is reduced to a page of footnotes. Yet the traditionalists, having assumed unverifiable premises, will go on to explain the inexplicable. First they posit a God who is beyond all human understanding, and then they proceed to discourse on his nature and purposes as if he were a next-door neighbor. Could anything be more puerile, for example, than the statement of the Bishop of London at the time of the first World War: "Do not blame God for this war; it is the work of Satan, who is constantly thwarting God's purposes." Of course, neither God nor Satan is to be blamed for war. Only men are to be blamed; only the greed, the hatred, the thirst for glory and the lust for power which poison the human mind.

There are three constant components of established religions. The first is the transmission of a faith embodied in the official creeds of the churches. The second is a form of worship, ranging from the elaborate mystical ritual of the Roman Church to the bare and bleak service of the cold, hard-seated puritan meetinghouse. The third (to which the first two are supposed to furnish the incentive) is the encouragement of a righteous life. These elements may be called respectively the doctrinal, the ceremonial, and the ethical components of religion; or, to give them their theological names, the didactic, the proskynetic, and the paraenetic. They are listed here in the order of their importance in the eyes of the church.

Now it seems to me that the order of these three components of religion ought to be exactly reversed. The doctrinal part, being as it is a mass of contradictory and inscrutable propositions upon which the sects have never agreed and never can agree, should be relegated to a position of insignificance. The creeds are interesting historical documents illustrating various stages in the development of civilization, and should be treated like their contemporary theories of science. They embody what was believed to be truth by the men who framed them, whose sincerity we can acknowledge, while we reject their premises and their conclusions. For example, the conception of

A RELIGION FOR ADULTS

God has grown as the spirit of man has widened. God has had a history, as truly as Julius Caesar. From a tribal deity of Mount Sinai, he developed into the absolute despot patterned on the oriental monarchs, and then into the majestic embodiment of righteousness of the Hebrew prophets, and finally into the loving father of all mankind preached by Jesus. He will ever be for us mortals, with our limited knowledge, a symbol for the highest aspirations of which we are capable. There is profound truth in the remark of Robert G. Ingersoll: "An honest God is the noblest work of man." Therefore, to transmit as a faith necessary to salvation dogmas founded on immature and unworthy conceptions of, God prevalent in past ages seems to me a fruitless and even a harmful procedure. The whole mass of unintelligible controversial doctrines which make up what Santayana called "the epic of salvation" should be divested of its alleged sacred authority and take its place among the historical survivals of man's early conceptions of science, philosophy and social duties.

As to ceremonialism, the form of worship in which we express our response to the emotional urge to supplement our ignorance by better knowledge, our weakness by firmer strength, and our moral failures by worthier conduct, that will vary according to the individual's taste. Some like ritual, and some do not. For some incense is a sweet aroma, and for others it is an offense to the nostrils. "Some," says Emily Dickinson, "keep the Sabbath by going to church, I keep it staying at home." That there is mutual helpfulness in the assembling of people to seek the highest in common counsel and meditation I fully believe. Above the platform of our meetinghouse in New York is the motto: "The place where men meet to seek the highest is holy ground." But there are many fine souls who have not found this communion necessary to their spiritual peace and progress. Worship, we must remember, is literally "worthship," and it is only as worship has this moral quality of worth that it is of significance. We can only say on this point: Each one according to his need. Worship, then, or the *form* in which men's highest aspirations are expressed, seems to me to be what the old moral philosophers called an "adiaphoron"—that is, a matter of minor importance *per se*.

The third component of religion, however, is all-important. It should be raised to the first place. For in the last analysis every religion above the crude appeals to the gods to ward off evils or bestow favors has had as its object the improvement of mankind. For what else does a church exist? And is it not strange that this primary objective of religion should have been obscured by dogma and ceremony and made contingent on these secondary factors? Instead of meeting together to give allegiance to creeds or to perform a ritual, we should meet to seek clarification and co-operation in the task of learning and performing our duties as ethical beings. Instead of leaving this all-important task to the individual, to be inferred from his doctrinal instruction, we should make it a prime concern of our communion together, leaving the questions of supernatural beliefs and ceremonial performances to the preference of the individual. This is not to eliminate religion, but to make it truly operative. It is not to deny the mystical element which will always be present in religion, but to recognize that it is not to be explained by doctrines which, like the Bishop of London's theory of the battle between God and Satan, leave more to be explained than they explain themselves. It is a monstrous assumption that because we cannot accept nonsensical "solutions" of problems, we therefore do not see the problems. As well say that if we reject a patent medicine nostrum for the cure of a disease we deny the existence of the disease. Yet that is what in effect the fundamentalist says when he insists on his remedy for evil. One would think that there was no such thing as awe and reverence except in the realm of illusion—which is the realm of immaturity.

Finally, it is characteristic of institutionalized religion, as of institutions generally, to lose the initial fervor of its founders and degenerate into fixed forms. This always means the reversion to traditional, and hence immature, conceptions and practices. The spirit is sacrificed to the form. Napoleon Bonaparte began his career as an ardent champion of the ideas of liberty, equality and fraternity as announced by the French Revolution. He gradually lost this idealism and used the power he had gained by his victories in war to establish himself as a despot, reviving the old abuses against which he had once fought. He restored the throne in its alliance with the altar. He brought the pope to Notre Dame and took from his hands the imperial crown to place on his own head.

ETHICS AS A RELIGION

When the pageant of reaction was over and the emperor was descending the steps of the cathedral with one of his old generals who had fought with him on many a battlefield of Europe for the liberation of the people from the autocratic sovereigns, he said to the general, "Was it not grand?" "Yes, sire," replied the old soldier, "except for the hundreds of thousands who died in order to do away with all this."

How many reformers and prophets have suffered persecution and martyrdom in their efforts to do away with the cramping survivals of religious infantilism! How childish do the trappings of orthodoxy seem to the mature mind! How eagerly do the traditionalists and the fundamentalists cling to the doctrines and forms of religion which have lost their power to enlist the hearty support of modem man! Is it not high time that we unite in the endeavor to define and practice a religion for adults?

CHAPTER TEN

ETHICAL FELLOWSHIP

One of the foremost sociologists of America, the late Professor Franklin H. Giddings of Columbia University, found the key to human behavior in what he called "the consciousness of kind." By that he meant that the most potent influence in determining the groupings of people in society was a sense of belonging, through a common conviction or preference, to this or that company of fellow beings. A Roman poet two thousand years ago expressed the same idea in the line, "To love the same things and hate the same things, this is genuine fellowship." And we endorse Professor Giddings' formula in our common proverb, "Birds of a feather flock together."

Only, we must distinguish carefully between the flocking together of birds of the same feather or beasts of the same species in the animal world and the groupings of human beings. It is inaccurate to speak of "societies" of bees and ants; for in the subhuman world it is an instinctive and inevitable bond that unites species in their behavior. No choice is exercised by them. They are condemned by nature to repeat from age to age, each species after its kind, the patterns of behavior peculiar to that species. We human beings, to be sure, share the instincts of the animal world on certain lower levels of behavior, such as response to the promptings of hunger, sleep, reproduction, clinging to life, and other unconscious and unreasoned responses to stimuli. But what distinguishes us fundamentally from the animals is the choice which we exercise in our social relations. There we rise to higher levels, and our affinities, to use Goethe's phrase, are "elective" and not instinctive. As that wonderfully gifted seeress Emily Dickinson put it:

The soul selects her own society,
Then shuts the door;
On her divine majority
Obtrude no more. . . .

ETHICAL FELLOWSHIP

I've known her from an ample nation
Choose one;
Then close the valves of her attention
Like stone.

Having this choice of the kind of company we shall keep and of the ideals and institutions to which we shall give our allegiance, there is a great responsibility put upon us to cherish that company and support those institutions by the contribution of such talents as we possess. For what a man prizes as his own highest ideal he will rejoice to see others sharing. He will wish to be associated with them so as to further his own and their endeavors. This is true fellowship. The word has a noble content, in the fellowship of scientists, artists, educators and religious believers.

But, alas, the word is too often used in common parlance to denote a spurious and conventional contact, not of serious purpose but of ephemeral chance acquaintance. There is a "hail fellow, well met" attitude and the "for he's a jolly good fellow" song which often have no element of real fellowship in them. Hardly anything is more distressing than to see people trying to persuade themselves that they are united in a band of brothers because they are singing "Oh, Eliza" at a Rotary Club luncheon. The indictment against this spurious fellowship is that it is not related to a common devotion to the highest moral ends or nourished by a reciprocal elicitation of the finest qualities of character. Minds too often meet on the lower levels of gossip about their neighbors. Conversation fails to rise above the stock market or the perversities of servants.

ETHICS AS A RELIGION

How seldom are the real issues of life discussed outside the pulpit or the platform address, and then how often are they treated in a perfunctory manner. Yet, in our brief journey through life all the subjects over which we get excited—money-making, labor strife, politics, prices, taxes—sink into insignificance as compared with the earnest cultivation of a character devoid of offense against man and God.

To further our efforts in this supreme task of life there is nothing more helpful than association with like-minded people in the quest for more light on our duty and more strength of will to perform it. I know that there are wide differences among men in the degree of need they feel for such association. Some will say, Why should I identify myself with a church or temple or Ethical Society? Can I not just as well sit comfortably at home and read an edifying book? Others, having found a former connection with a religious body unsatisfactory, will hesitate to join another group, fearing to "put their head in a noose" again. Thousands who join all sorts of clubs for their pleasure or social standing in the community (for we are the greatest nation of "joiners" on earth) feel no obligation to unite with a group which is devoted to the cultivation of ethical practices. Yet their need for such spiritual companionship, if they but realized it, is greater than their need for physical recreation or even mental improvement. Aristotle's dictum of twenty-three hundred years ago is still true, that man is a social being. He may develop a talent in solitude, but only in the process of life mingling with

ETHICAL FELLOWSHIP

life can he form a character. In the very atmosphere of the meeting of people like-minded in the pursuit of spiritual edification there is "something added" beyond what any one of the participants brings. The whole here is greater than the sum of the parts. The chord is more than the combination of the separate notes. Even in the silent Quaker service there is eloquence in the aura of stillness. In the little New England town in which I was brought up there was an elderly woman whose presence was like a benediction. She had more misfortune to bear than falls to the lot of most people: grinding poverty, an improvident husband, the care of six growing children, the frustration, through unrelieved drudgery, of the cultivation and expression of genuine intellectual gifts. Yet when she put on her one black dress and went to the village church on Sunday, she left her cares behind. "I don't mind so much what the minister talks about," she would say, "but I feel refreshed and strengthened by just sitting with my fellow worshipers and singing the hymns." For her, as for many like her, the hour of devotional attitude in itself was a spiritual tonic. There was no doctrinal or controversial element in it. The sense of silent communion with other seekers for spiritual strength was enough.

Now, there are thousands and thousands of men and women in our land who are not affiliated with church or temple; and thousands more whose affiliation is of the most tenuous sort. On certain occasions, like funerals or weddings, they avail themselves of the services of priest, minister or rabbi. Sometimes they go to places of worship.

ETHICS AS A RELIGION

I had a friend who used to say facetiously that he went to church "regularly"—every Easter. These people have no focus of spiritual life. They live in the dim penumbra of religious conventionality. They dwell in the great religious valley of indecision. It is to these masses of the unchurched that our Ethical Societies offer a fellowship which we believe has inestimable value. We do not seek to win from their allegiance to the Jewish or Christian faith those people who are spiritually satisfied with the creeds and ceremonies of the churches and temples. We are not proselyters. We only offer the kind of religious fellowship which we have found exceedingly precious in our own lives, and which, in the missionary spirit of the desire to share our experience with others, we recommend to those who are seeking in this confused and materialistic age a solution for the persistent questions of the meaning of life and the claims of duty.

Let me, then, as best I can, set forth some of the values which we find and prize in our ethical fellowship. First of all, it is a religious fellowship. Although we engage in many activities, educational, charitable, and social—such as the Ethical Culture Schools, play schools, summer camps, neighborhood settlements, adult educational programs, etc.—all these activities are inspired and guided by a deep religious purpose. They are the outgrowth and expression of a faith in the sacredness of the human individual and in his duty and capacity so to use his contacts with his fellow men as to encourage in them and in himself the development of latent qualities of nobility. From the very inception of our movement these activities have been regarded not as ends in themselves but as instrumental to the larger end of creating a community of mutually stimulating seekers after righteousness; what the early Christian baptismal formula called "the community of saints" and the founder of our movement called "the ethical manifold." In all his valuable contributions to humanitarian causes, such as tenement house reform, abolition of child labor, encouragement of progressive education, mediation of labor disputes, the crusade against commercialized vice, Felix Adler was constantly motivated by his faith in the inherent and indefeasible dignity of man. If this dignity were recognized and respected in society at large, the evils which disgrace our age would disappear. Racial prejudice, religious intolerance, economic exploitation, political corruption would give way to brotherhood, justice, honesty and mercy. Wars would cease and the rumors of wars be stilled. Granted that this is a "consummation devoutly to be wished" rather than a goal promising speedy attainment, the fact does not invalidate the ideal. Rather does it strengthen it. For unless the ideal is kept high the zeal to grapple with conditions which threaten it is dampened. The alternative to perfection is not pessimism or cynicism, but meliorism. The pure light of the ideal is broken by the prism of actuality into varied hues; or, as Shelley so beautifully says in his "Adonais":

> *Life, like a dome of many-colored glass,*
> *Stains the white radiance of eternity.*

ETHICS AS A RELIGION

Our work must lie in this world of tragic imperfection; but our gaze must be fixed on the pattern of perfection revealed to us by the eye of faith. We cannot reach the stars; but we can steer by them.

Our brethren in church and synagogue are generally loath to regard the Ethical Societies as a religious fellowship. How can you speak of religion, they say, when you have no creed or litany, no sacred authoritative scriptures, no ordained priesthood or ministry, no sacraments? Without any desire to enter into a polemic on these points (for religious arguments are likely to be futile) I would only suggest that all these alleged essentials of religion are but the accessories of religion, varying widely, as the creeds and ceremonies prove, from age to age and from clime to clime. They do not create religion, as so many believe, but are themselves the creations of religion. There have been countless attempts by philosophers and theologians to define religion. There have been countless manifestations of religion, ranging from the tom-tom beating and totem worship of the savage, the sacrifice of animals and human beings, nature myths, magic-mongering, mystic rites, to the ethical monotheism of the Hebrew prophets and the universalism of the message of Jesus. Havelock Ellis tells us that in certain African tribes the question put to a stranger was, "What religion do you dance?" One must be singularly blind to the revolutionary changes which the discoveries of science and the study of comparative religions, the urge of democracy and the growth of the spirit of humanism have wrought in the faith of our grandfathers not to recognize that the champions of an infallible authority in book or hierarchy are fighting a losing battle in the religious world, just as the champions of an infallible political authority in a king or *Führer* have striven in vain to hold back the tide of democracy. There are still plenty of ecclesiastical Canutes seated on the shore and bidding the advancing waves of a rational humanitarian faith to stay their rise. It is a futile gesture. The world moves forward and "the thoughts of men are widened with the suns." We must constantly purge our religious inheritance, as we do our historical, scientific, medical, educational and other cultural inheritances, of the detritus of myth, magic and mandate which is carried down the stream of time from former ages of fixed prescription and custom.

Now, when we relegate to their appropriate subordinate place all the trappings and accretions of religion, we discover the heart of religion to be in the complete devotion of an individual to the search for light on his duties to his fellow men and the discipline of his will to perform those duties to the best of his abilities. It is a simple definition, needing no theological elaboration. But it is the definition of a task of infinite difficulty to fulfill. We of the Ethical Societies are pledged to the unceasing effort to fulfill that task. On the tablet on the outside of our meetinghouse in New York are inscribed the words, "Dedicated to the ever increasing knowledge, love and practice of the right." Again, above our platform in the meetinghouse one reads the inscription, "The place where men meet to seek the

ETHICS AS A RELIGION

highest is holy ground." But do not the churches and the temples also require right conduct and the spirit of reverence? Certainly they do. But the point on which we differ from them is a point of emphasis. They place correct belief first and derive moral conduct from religious faith, while we find in the appeal of moral conduct itself a sufficient motive. Ethics is for them, as it were, a satellite deriving its light from a theological sun. For us ethics is the sun itself, the source of all the light that has guided man's faltering footsteps in this world. It is the basis on which all the creeds have been built and the factor which gives to any religion worthy of the name its dignity and authority. We call our ethical fellowship a religious fellowship, therefore, because in ethics we find the heart and core of religion.

In the second place, our fellowship is a fellowship of freedom. The sole condition of membership is the desire to be associated with a group devoted to ethical culture—that is, to the cultivation of moral character. We do not ask what views a person holds on the existence of God or the person of Christ or the immortality of the soul, knowing that these are speculative questions on which men have argued differently and vainly for centuries. We have no creed or litany; but we have a burning faith, the faith in man's capacity to shape his own spiritual destiny by the force of a will enlightened by reason and fortified by resolve. No one speaks from our platform in the language of "Thus saith the Lord"; but we seek as a democratic cooperative group to encourage one another in devotion to our ethical duty. What a joyous relief it is when the burden of the effort to reconcile incomprehensible dogmas rolls off the mind and one is free from the conflict between .faith and reason. For freedom is the only condition in the religious as in the political sphere under which mankind can progress toward the realization of his ideals. "I have sworn on the altar of God," wrote Thomas Jefferson to Benjamin Rush, "eternal enmity against every form of tyranny over the mind of man."

But the freedom which we value in our ethical fellowship means more than mere release from the trammels of dogmas which have held so many minds in bondage. This is not an end in itself, but only the prerequisite for the beneficent use of our freedom. The various educational and charitable activities of our Societies to which I have alluded are the manifestations of our sense of responsibility for such use. To employ the language of the theologians, they are "the outward and visible signs of an inward and spiritual grace." They are all undertaken as the exemplification of a spiritual conviction: namely, that our own freedom is inextricably linked with the freedom of our fellow men. What a striking confirmation of this truth has been shown to our complacent people by the terrible wars of the twentieth century! We thought that we could remain free, secure and prosperous while the rest of the world was torn with strife. "Let them stew in their own juice" was the slogan of the smug isolationists. There was something of the spirit of the grim old church father Tertullian, who pictured the joy of the saints in heaven leaning over the battlements to rejoice in the tortures of sinners writhing in hell. But we have learned by bitter experience that peace and security are as "indivisible" as war. When President Roosevelt declared in his Chicago speech of October, 1937, that a *cordon sanitaire* must be drawn around the nations which were bent on wrecking the world's freedom, he was roundly abused in this country as a "war-monger" himself. Colonel Robert McCormick's *Tribune* displayed a sign just across the avenue from the President's platform, reading: "We are not alarmed." The majority of Americans seemed to refuse to believe that Nazi and Nipponese doctrines were contagious, in spite of the witness of fifth columns and poisonous propaganda in the countries where the evil had already spread.

Emerson has told us that the man who holds one end of a chain which binds a slave at the other end is himself held in bondage, for we are members one of another. In the middle years of the last century, for example, a courageous fight was waged by the advocates of free public education against the privileged classes who could not see why they should pay taxes for the schooling of other people's children. They were blind to the fact that a generation growing up in ignorance and unprotected against the temptations to lawlessness was a greater threat to their own security than the comparatively small demands which the cost of schools and teachers would make on their pocketbooks. They took the attitude of the priest and the Levite in the parable of the good Samaritan, content to go their own way and pass up a need which they mistakenly thought was none of their business. The mistake of such isolationism from a social duty is far different from, say, an error in adding up a column of figures. In the latter case one has no sense of guilt. One simply tries again and gets the right result. But if one omits the duty of response to a humanitarian appeal a haunting feeling of shame may disturb one's peace for days.

The freedom which we prize in our ethical fellowship, then, is not solely or even chiefly liberation *from* the mental embarrassment of the "gnawing worm of religious uncertainty" fed by conflicting creeds; it is rather a liberation *for* the use of such talents as we have in the common task of eliminating the evils of prejudice, greed, pride and violence from the behavior of men and nations. We are under no illusions as to the difficulties of this task. We know that what any one of us, or a small company of us, can do for the accomplishment of this task will be but a small contribution. But the result of our endeavor is not the measure of our duty. Nor do we know how far a little candle may cast its beam. At any rate we can light our little candle and set it firmly on its iron point, as the pious Catholic does in his cathedral; he to honor his patron saint, and we to help light the road to human brotherhood. In a word, paradoxical as it may seem, our freedom is born of the sense of obligation. We are truly liberated when we become conscious of our involvement in the liberty of our fellows. So long as there is slavery we are not free ourselves. So long as racial hatred and persecution exists we too are its victims. So long as ignorance darkens any part of our land we are dwelling in its shadow. We ourselves build the "stone walls and iron bars" of Richard Lovelace's familiar lines when we hem in our sympathy for those who are bound by the fetters of ignorance and oppression.

> *If I have freedom in my love,*
> *And in my soul am free,*
> *Angels alone, that soar above,*
> *Enjoy such liberty.*

A third value of our ethical fellowship is its devotion to an ideal rather than to any person, however exalted he may be. It is a fellowship and not a fellowship. This is a crucial point on which we differ from other religious groups. They emphasize the idea of a mediator in the form of a priest or lawgiver or redeemer through whose offices alone man may set his feet on the path of salvation. We would not yield to the most orthodox Christian or Jew in our appreciation of the inspiration which the lives and teachings of the great apostles of righteousness from the Hebrew prophets to Jesus of Nazareth have been for mankind. But we think of them not as figures to be worshiped but rather as themselves worshipers with us of an ideal which enlisted all of their, and should enlist all of our, devotion. I know that this is a counsel of perfection. We are constantly told that men cannot rise to the comprehension of an ideal unless they see it incarnated in a person. But if we made the worship of a person the test of religion, we should have to eliminate from the list of worthies some of the noblest names the world has ever known—a Gautama, a Spinoza, a Giordano Bruno, a Jefferson, an Emerson, a Lincoln.

Let us then in thankful humility acknowledge the blessings which we have derived from the world's great exemplars of religion; but let us not accept their merits in lieu of our own responsibilities or plead their strength to ex- . tenuate our own weakness. No true religious teacher asks for the worship of his own person. What he seeks is a company of worshipers of his ideals.

There are two common criticisms of our ethical fellowship that I would notice before closing this chapter. Some say, Your meetings are cold; they are too much dominated by intellectual discourse; they lack the appeal to emotion which is the chief element in religion. It is true that we lay little stress on the external features of worship. We have no robed choirs or recited prayers. Those who crave such stimuli to the good life will find them aplenty in the ceremonies of the churches. But it seems to me that none except those who come to our meetings with coldness in their own hearts could find the ethical faith which we preach bleak and barren. Ought anything that appeals to the sensuous emotions of color or sound or smell kindle in us a warmth equal to that of meeting to seek together new light on the path of duty? Though we do not regard devotion to intellectual clarity as a reproach, we nevertheless hold the intellect to be but the tool which we use for shaping the end and purpose of ethical improvement. That purpose can and does irradiate the souls of men and women who are intent upon it with a warmth which no external ceremony can provide.

Another criticism of our ethical fellowship is that it must fail to furnish comfort and support in times of sorrow and bereavement. This is a matter which cannot be decided by argument, but only by actual experience. We are all subject to the frustrations of life. Hopes are unrealized, sickness lays us low, friends and loved ones are taken from us, and we know that we must follow them into the great silence. Each of us must find in his own soul the degree of fortitude or weakness with which he meets these inevitable frustrations. All that I would say on this subject of poignancy is that I am convinced that the ethical religion has furnished as much courage and comfort to its followers in times of trouble as any devotee of Christianity has received from priest or minister. In the noble words of the close of his *An Ethical Philosophy of Life* Felix Adler wrote: "As my last act I affirm that the ideal of perfection which my mind inevitably conceives has its counterpart in the ultimate reality of things. . . . I affirm that there verily is an eternal divine life, a best beyond the best that I can think or imagine, in which all that is best in me and best in those who are dear to me is contained and continued. In this sense I bless the universe. And to be able to bless the universe in one's last moments is the supreme prize which man can wrest from life's struggles and life's experiences." Measuring faith with faith, I find such heroic resignation far more comforting than the fantastic argument of St. Paul for the resurrection of the body, in the fifteenth chapter of the first Epistle to the Corinthians. Ethical religion *can* say to its disciples in time of trial, "My grace is sufficient for thee." According to the story in the Gospels Jesus raised from the dead the son of the widow of Nain. According to the Buddhist scriptures when one came to the master saying, "My son is dead," he replied, "Go through the village and ask for a grain of millet in every house into which sorrow has not entered." And the searcher came back at evening empty-handed. Is there more comfort in the alleged miracle than in the Buddhist parable?

CHAPTER ELEVEN

THE POSTULATES OF ETHICAL RELIGION

IN AN EARLIER CHAPTER (Seven) we noted the two chief works of the German philosopher Immanuel Kant: namely, the *Critique of Pure Reason* and the *Critique of Practical Reason.* In the former Kant devoted several hundred laborious pages to the demonstration of the obvious fact that the human intellect cannot grasp

THE POSTULATES OF ETHICAL RELIGION

what is beyond its grasp. In the latter, moved as we have seen by the emotions of reverence implanted by his pietistic mother and "roused from his dogmatic slumbers" by the skepticism of David Hume, he sought to show that the existence of God, the immortality of the soul and a state of future rewards and punishments after death were propositions that had to be accepted as true, in spite of the inability of the mind to demonstrate them logically. These propositions he called "postulates" (from the Latin *postulare,* to demand), since, although they were not objects of knowledge, they demanded our assent as having a necessary meaning for our "practice." Quite apart from any exercise of logic, we must act, he maintained, as if God existed and virtue and vice would receive their due reward in a future state. For this shift from the ground of rigorous logic to that of supralogical faith Kant has been accused by some critics of a cowardly desertion of intellectual integrity, while others have praised him for recognizing that undemonstrable beliefs may have a reality for us which transcends pure reason.

Nor is it in the field of religion alone that men act on postulates. The believer in a democratic form of government postulates the eventual happiness and prosperity of a political regime founded on the active co-operation of free citizens in their rights and duties. The autocrat, on the other hand, postulates the beneficence of a regime in which a supreme ruler determines what is good for his subjects and enforces his will not by persuasion but by coercion. No abstract reasoning can shake the faith of the believer in either of these political postulates. One school of economic theory postulates the general advantage of a system of competitive individual initiative, with no interference, or at least a minimum of interference, by the government; while another school insists that the public will be better served by a system in which the production and distribution of the country's wealth is taken out of the hands of the individual entrepreneurs and given over to agencies of the state. Again, as in the case of political regimes, there is no metaphysical arbitrament of these conflicting economic faiths. So it is, I think, with theories of education, canons of art, types of literature. All rest on postulates: that is, on the assumption of the beneficence of their particular contribution to the field of activity in which they are exercised.

Now, ethical religion, like the religions of creed and ceremony, rests on certain postulates or assumptions which are as necessary to its theory and practice as are the postulates of orthodoxy. It is no mere list of moral precepts. It has rootage in a philosophy which underlies and determines specific acts of conduct. One day a hostile critic of our ethical movement said to me, "Your Ethical Societies are commendable for their earnestness and good works; but after all they fail to substantiate their claim to be a religion. They are like 'cut flowers,' without roots in the soil of tradition. They will therefore wither ere long for lack of spiritual nourishment." How wrong this judgment was I hope to show in the following discussion of the postulates on which our ethical religion rests. In some respects they will be identical with the postulates of Judaism and Christianity, and in other respects they will depart in substance or in emphasis from them. These aspects of identity and contrast will be kept in mind during the discussion.

The first postulate of ethical religion is the existence of a moral law in the universe, as permeating and indefeasible as the physical laws of nature. Belief in this moral law far antedates the rise of Christianity. Thousands of years ago the Egyptian sages recognized the binding force of this law, as we see from the pyramid texts and ethical precepts recorded in the late Professor Breasted's fascinating book, *The Dawn of Conscience.* For the Hebrews in their crude tribal state Jehovah was a local god of battles like the gods of neighboring tribes; but for the great prophets of Israel he became the incarnation of universal moral law. More than four centuries before the birth of Jesus the Greek tragedian Sophocles makes his heroine Antigone stand fearlessly up to King Creon and invoke, in justification of her defiance, a higher law than the king's edict: "Nor deemed I that thy decrees were of such force that a mortal could override the unwritten and unfailing statutes of heaven. For their life is not of yesterday or today, but from all time, and no man knows when they were first put forth." What were these "statutes of heaven" which Egyptian, Israelite and Greek long centuries ago, as well as Wordsworth and Emerson and Gandhi in recent times, have seen as binding on the conscience of man, but the majestic moral law which pervades the universe? It is the matrix of all just laws of mortal making. It is, in the language of Plato, the "idea" of law itself, "laid up in heaven"; transcendent, indefinable, inexorable, but so *real* to believing men that they have gone to the stake, faced wild beasts in the arena, and drunk the hemlock rather than disobey its commands.

But do not the synagogues and churches also exalt the moral law? Do they not also postulate a binding sense of obligation on the part of men to live up to its commands to the limit of their possibilities? Certainly they do. Yet there is a real difference between the postulate of moral law as held by synagogue and church and that held by the ethical religion. And the difference lies in the fact that for Judaism and Christianity the source of the moral law lies in certain historical events which seem to the Ethical Culturist to qualify, or to tend to qualify, its universality. For example, in Judaism it is the "Law of Moses"—the Torah and its supplements and commentaries— that gives a tone of particularism to moral law. The concept of a "chosen people," in spite of the injunction laid upon them to consider their "election" to Jehovah's favor as a mission to extend his commands to nations of the world, affects the moral law with an element of prescribed historic ritual which limits rather than commends its universality. Turn back, if you please, to the words of Joseph Klausner quoted near the beginning of Chapter Three and see the traces of racialism and legalism which still linger in the Jewish conception of the reign of moral law. Though the nations are not literally to be gathered to the holy hill of

THE POSTULATES OF ETHICAL RELIGION

Zion, yet "the historic national culture" of the Jewish people is to continue, "the politico-spiritual Messianic ideal of Israel" is to be realized "in all its fulness," and the "ceremonial laws of Judaism . . . shall not be altogether abolished, since they serve to protect the existence of the nation." This is hardly the language of a universal moral law which transcends the accidents of race or ritual.

Nor does the Christian conception of the moral law wholly satisfy our ethical demands. This is because the Christianity (or perhaps one should say the "churchianity") developed by the church fathers and councils conditioned acceptable moral conduct upon theological belief. Emerson was ostracized by the Harvard Divinity School because in his address of 1838 to the students he declared that nothing was at last sacred to them but the integrity of their own minds. Virtue was virtue, from whatever source it came. But in the eyes of the church the virtues of the man who did not confess to having been "born again" by the grace of God were only manifestations of mundane pride.

This interposition of a theological sanction detracted from the majesty of moral law. For it made its universal and timeless authority, so magnificently stated in the plea of Antigone which we have quoted, subordinate to the authority of a dogma imposed by an institution which had grown to power in the midst of historical vicissitudes that greatly modified its primitive character. But ethics is independent of theological creeds. The universal moral law admits no impediment to its validity, no modification of its authority. It contains its own sanction.

A second postulate of ethical religion is the existence of a spiritual element in man's nature which makes him capable of seeking the fulfillment of the moral law in his daily conduct. It is on the ground of that capability that we attribute worth to him. And it is to that capability that the appeal of every worthy religion has been made. Certainly this was true of the religion taught by the Hebrew prophets and by Jesus. The latter throughout his ministry never ceased to exhort and *expect* men to turn from evil to righteousness. All his wonderful parables (the prodigal son, the good Samaritan, the friend at midnight, the workers in the vineyard, and the rest) were told to stimulate in his hearers the resolve to lead a better life. In the Sermon on the Mount there is not a single proposition of theological tenor; the "blessed" are those who manifest the *ethical* qualities of humility, purity of soul, love of peace, and hunger and thirst after righteousness.

How did it come about that the wholesome confidence in man's mental and moral capacities which characterized the great thinkers of antiquity, like Socrates, Plato, Aristotle, Epictetus and Seneca, yielded to the despairing doctrine of human impotence to cope with the challenge of destiny or take a single step toward spiritual growth? Gilbert Murray, in his *Five Stages of Greek Religion,* coined the phrase "the failure of nerve" to designate the period of intellectual and moral letdown that followed the age of Aristotle and Alexander the Great. The zest for construc-

THE POSTULATES OF ETHICAL RELIGION

tive thinking was lost. Men lived on the leavings of great ages past. A soul-sickness spread like an epidemic, and the cult of savior-gods flourished in all parts of the Roman Empire. It was in this soil of intellectual and moral abdication that the seed of Christianity was sown. And the theologians of the early church, inevitably influenced by the "climate of opinion" of the age in which they lived, erected the doctrine of man's utter incompetence to enter on the path of righteousness except through the grace of the one Savior-God into the basic dogma of the church. If protests against the denial of the efficacy of man's own will and reason to guide him in the search for righteousness were raised here and there, they were silenced by the authority of the church. Thus, when an Irish monk named Pelagius asserted that man could take the initiative in procuring his salvation through good works, he was condemned as a heretic by St. Augustine in a blistering treatise against Pelagianism. Nor were the Protestant reformers like Luther and Calvin any less firm in their denunciation of the doctrine of man's competence, in his "natural" state of sin, to move toward virtue. The moral of the parable of the prodigal son escaped them.

Closely allied to the ethical postulate of man's capacity through the constant exercise of will to set his feet on the path of righteousness, or, in Tennyson's language, "to rise on stepping stones of his dead self to better things," is his responsibility to demonstrate that capacity in his relations with his fellow men. There is no doubt that religion is the most important concern of our lives; but because religion has so generally been conceived of as making one's peace with God and so ensuring an eternity of bliss, the attention of men has been withdrawn from the give-and-take relations with their fellows and centered on their own state of soul. Witness the vast number of men and women who have renounced all contact with society and secluded themselves in monasteries or nunneries to spend their lives in meditation, prayer and holy exercises which have the sole purpose of preparing them to "meet their God." And even when, like the Puritans, for example, they have remained "in the world," they have directed their whole effort toward warning men, women and even little children that their one awful duty was to keep constantly in mind that they must prepare for leaving the world. But there is something morbid and sickly in this excessive preoccupation with the state of one's soul, this continual worry over one's sins. Emerson called it "the soul's mumps, measles and whooping cough." William James, after recounting in his *Varieties of Religious Experience* cases of self-congratulation of men and women on attaining personal assurance of their favor with God, adds bluntly: "The pivot round which the religious life, as we have traced it, revolves is the interest of the individual in his private personal destiny. Religion, in short, is a monumental chapter in the history of human egotism. . . . Today, quite as much as at any previous age, the religious individual tells you that the divine meets him on the basis of his personal concerns." I am not saying that we should close our hearts to the inflow of religious strength which

THE POSTULATES OF ETHICAL RELIGION

we get from a reverent contemplation of the perfection manifested in "the starry heavens above and the moral law within." We can welcome these influences as truly as any St. Teresa or John of the Cross did. It is only the failure to let such inspiration flow out again into acts of justice and mercy toward our fellow men that merits reproof. A "cloistered virtue" is no virtue at all.

The two ethical postulates of the existence of a universal moral law and of the natural capacity and duty of man to advance toward the fulfillment of that law (the first of which is shared by orthodox religion, but not the second) have an important bearing on a subject not hitherto treated in these chapters: namely, prayer. Probably the feature of our Ethical meetings which accounts chiefly for the reluctance of the churches to recognize Ethical Culture as a religion is the absence of prayer from our services. Other forms of worship, such as responsive readings, congregational singing, and a period of silent meditation, are practiced by one or another of our Societies. Those which can afford it have an organ. Some have memorial windows. But no prayers, extemporaneous or prescribed, are offered from our platforms. Several years ago a fine man who had left the church joined our staff of leaders; but after a while he left us because, as he said, he missed the prayers. Emerson, on the other hand, left the church partly because he could not bring himself to pray in public every Sunday at eleven o'clock. There would seem to be little warrant in the teaching of Jesus for public prayer. Not only did he not offer any prayers in public, but he counseled his followers to enter their closets and pray in secret. He condemned the Pharisees who made long prayers before an audience. We know not what goes on in the minds of our congregations, but it is likely that a prayerful attitude is more common than we think; especially if we interpret prayer in the sense of the poet as "the soul's desire, uttered or unexpressed." But it is not a question of this silent aspiration that we are discussing here. That it is a source of strength and comfort to many a worshiper is beyond doubt. It conflicts in no wise with our ethical postulates. However, when it comes to formal uttered prayers the case is different.

First of all, petitions to God for public or private favors are inconsistent with the ethical postulate of inexorable law in both the physical and the moral universe. Such exercises were appropriate to a time when God was conceived of as a *deus ex machina,* who could be persuaded to intervene in emergencies to save a situation. The votive tablets affixed to the walls of churches mentioned in an earlier chapter, thanking God, or a saint, for some favor received, are an example of this kind of petitional prayer. I was told the story of a nervous woman on board of a ship in the midst of a severe storm. When she appealed to an officer to assure her of safety and was advised to pray, she answered, "Oh, dear, has it come to that?" The crasser forms of faith in the efficacy of prayers for the miraculous intervention of supernatural powers, such as we see in some countries today, have yielded in more enlightened lands to a saner and more scientific view of nature. We rely on medicine and not incantations to cure the sick. We no longer regard the insane as possessed by devils to be exorcised by holy rites. We do not organize processions bearing the effigy of a saint at their head to ward off an epidemic or produce rain. For all that, we have not wholly laid aside prayers in the churches for the intervention of God in the course of nature or in righting the wrongs caused by human folly. To pray for rain is nonsense. And to pray God to repair the damages done by man is a cowardly renunciation of human responsibility. Remember the true word of the Indian sage: "By man is evil done, and by man must evil be undone."

This is not to deny that prayer for strength and courage to correct the manifold evils with which our age is afflicted may have a reflex effect in stimulating us to better efforts. But that is its only utility. We must not "he down on God," under the comforting delusion that He will do our work. Thus the second ethical postulate of the capacity and duty of man to advance toward the fulfillment of the moral law of the universe is vindicated. Whatever value prayer (silent prayer) has in this human effort must be taken in the sense of obligation to our fellow men expressed in Portia's noble lines:

We do pray for mercy;
And that same prayer doth teach us all to render
The deeds of mercy.

A third postulate of ethical religion is the nondependence of ethics upon any philosophical or theological system. Philosophy has its roots in curiosity, "the thirst to know and understand." The philosopher has an analytical disposition. He is concerned with such questions as how the mind apprehends knowledge (epistemology) or how it operates in conjunction with brain, nerves, glands and other bodily factors (psychology). Such studies are objective. But religion has its roots in deeper soil. It springs from anxiety and often anguish of spirit. It is a quest for a satisfying answer to such questions as What shall I do to justify my endowment with reason and conscience? How shall I attain inward peace? Where shall I find strength to perform the duties to my fellows which are enjoined on me by the commands of conscience? Compared with these spiritual imperatives the speculations of philosophy seem remote and irrelevant. The contrast between philosophy and religion is illustrated in the chief work of the founder of the Ethical movement, *An Ethical Philosophy of Life*. Part Two of Felix Adler's book is devoted to "philosophical theory." The reader cannot fail to detect the difference between the metaphysical subtleties of this part and the sections of the book concerned with the ethical experiences and their application in the various relations of life. The latter have a fervor which we miss in the former. In fact, Dr. Adler says himself, "Persons who are not trained in metaphysical thinking or interested in it may do well to omit the reading of the second part." Being a deep philosophical thinker himself, he felt the need of a critical analysis of Immanuel Kant's thought, for example. But, as his recommendation just quoted shows, he

THE POSTULATES OF ETHICAL RELIGION

did not believe that for others such analysis was a necessary preparation or guide for living an ethical life. As for the nonindependence of ethics on theology, enough has been said in previous pages. One marvels at the persistence of the theory that belief in the dogmas of a creed is the necessary basis for ethical conduct. For however much the clergy in their official capacity may insist upon this theory, in their actual daily contacts with men they honor it more in the breach than in the observance. No .priest, rabbi or minister would fail to put more trust in an upright man who was a "nonbeliever" than in one who made a confession of faith that was not followed by "good works." A survey of the religious views of several hundred inmates of state prisons a few years ago revealed the fact that a very large percentage of them declared that they were Christians. This extreme case, of course, is not typical. It is cited only to show how much easier it is to profess a conventional religion than to be a religious person. Yet the church has unfortunately attached an undue importance to the confession of man's incompetence for righteousness and too little to his struggling though imperfect exemplification of it. An orthodox minister once said of the eminent Unitarian William E. Channing, "He is excluded from the highest form of religious life by the extraordinary rectitude of his character!"

In these times of awful world crisis the cry that goes out from all hearts is *Deliverance!*—deliverance from the haunting fear lest the devilish accumulation of lethal weapons which the nations are preparing for their defense

ETHICS AS A RELIGION

may lead to the destruction of a defenseless world; deliverance from the hunger and homelessness, the indignity and slavery, imposed on millions of innocent men, women and children by the will of power-crazed despots; deliverance from the repeated deadlocks of parleys and panels to substitute co-operation for mutual defiance in the field of labor-management relations, and to supplant the suspicion, jealousy, pride, and insufferable megalomania of the nations with a common recognition of their interdependence and a generous spirit of mutual respect; deliverance, finally, from the dry rot of materialism which is threatening the very disintegration of the principles of honor on which our country was founded, and bids fair to center our efforts on the acquirement of every possession except self-possession. Where shall we look for deliverance from these evils but in a new baptism of ethical religion? Appeals to supernatural powers have proved vain. Confidence in the efficacy of blueprints for the unity of mankind has waned. The road to sanity and security seems to be blocked with obstacles too heavy to be removed. Men hesitate between despair and "on with the dance." The churches offer the old bottles of dogma to hold the new wine of ethical ferment. The labels remain on the bottles, but the contents have evaporated. We cannot go back to Nicaea or Westminster for our religious inspiration today. That can come only from a devout reverence for human life. That phrase "reverence for life" was given us by a wonderful man who, in spite of the charges of heresy raised against him, dared to found his ethics not on theology (of which he was a master) but on "inspiring trust in the natural goodness of human nature." Let the words of Albert Schweitzer close our chapter: "Amid the babel of tongues that supervene on this period of humanity's most poignant distress, the ethics of Reverence for Life, if heard and heeded in its gentle undertones, would prove a far more efficacious remedy for the world's pains than all the panaceas advocated in strident tones by the politicians or the sociologists or the theologians."

CHAPTER TWELVE

OUR ETHICAL HERITAGE

THE WISE Goethe wrote, "What thou hast inherited from thy fathers, that thou must win in order to possess it." This truth is fully recognized by the scientists. Their magnificent achievements in physics, chemistry, medicine, engineering and a hundred other fields would not have been possible except for the accumulated knowledge of the past. If new data, more precise instruments, and above all fresh inspirations of genius made some of this knowledge obsolete, nevertheless the new knowledge was always a development of the old, and was itself subject to further amendment in the on-going search for truth. A Darwin could not have arrived at the new truth of evolution without working on and working out of the old accepted truth of the immutability of species. An Einstein could not have discovered the theory of relativity if he had not absorbed the knowledge of the mathematicians and the physicists of the past generations. The gifted band of scientists working to release the tremendous latent energy in the atom were building on the foundations laid by the Curies in the discovery of radium and by Dalton and others who furnished the scale of atomic weights. As it is with the scientist, so it is with the architect, the musician, the poet and the novelist. There are canons of taste and models of excellence which all except the cranks who produce mere noise and call it music or write meaningless jargon which they call poetry are bound to observe.

Why is it that the scientists are so ready to acknowledge the provisional nature of the work of their predecessors (and indeed of their own) while in the field of religion there is so much resistance to new interpretations? The reason is not far to seek. It is because science has freed itself from the trammels of a fixed and final authority. This has not been an easy task. Only a few centuries ago the church, on the basis of truth as revealed in the Bible, claimed jurisdiction over men's research in astronomy, geology, biology and all other branches of science. Witness Galileo, compelled on his knees to renounce the theory of the earth's movement; Giordano Bruno, burned at the stake because he taught the doctrine of the infinitude of the universe; Darwin and Wallace, branded as the robbers of man's spiritual birthright by demonstrating his physical kinship with the lower forms of animal life; Hutton and Lyell, condemned as heretics because they extended the existence of the earth from the creation week of the book of Genesis to hundreds of millions of years. Now the battle for the freedom of scientific inquiry is won. Even the most orthodox sects have abandoned the chronology of Genesis and ceased to combat the doctrine of evolution. But even the liberal churches are as yet far from conceding the provisional nature of the religious creeds which were formulated in the same days of scientific ignorance and hallowed custom. The feasts of Judaism which mark the people of Israel as a chosen people are still kept. The Christian ceremonies which endorse the plan of a vicarious salvation are still celebrated. Clergymen of all sects are still pledged to confine their intellectual explorations within the limits of divinely revealed truth. This is the crux of the present situation in religion. So long as the would-be innovator in science was compelled to operate with respect to finalities set down by an Aristotle, a Galen or a church council, there could be no advance in philosophy, medicine or astronomy. Likewise the progress toward a unifying and humanistic religion will be hampered so long as men's minds are not completely free to criticize, amend and reject any religious doctrine held sacred in the past. The dead hand of bondage to tradition still weighs upon us. We are not at the meridian but at the cock-crow dawn of civilization, as Emerson wrote a century ago. We are still at the dawn of religious freedom, which is basic to all other freedoms of the race. And unless we win the battle for a religion which transcends the parochialism of Judaism and Christianity, we shall in vain hope for the unity of mankind, which is the requisite for a peaceful world.

The venerable John Dewey in his little book *A Common Faith* writes:

> "We who now live are parts of a humanity that extends into a remote past, a humanity that has interacted with nature. The things in civilization we most prize are not of ourselves. They exist by grace of the doings and sufferings of the continuous human community in which we are a link. Ours is the responsibility of conserving, transmitting, rectifying and expanding the heritage of values we have received, that those who come after us may receive it more solid and more secure, more widely accessible and more generously shared than we have received it. Here are all the elements for a religious faith which shall not be confined to sect, class or race. Such a faith has always been implicitly the common faith of mankind. It remains to make it explicit and militant."

ETHICS AS A RELIGION

That is the meaning of Goethe's words quoted at the beginning of this chapter. A man may inherit money, houses and land from a rich father without any merit or effort on his own part. Material goods can be hoarded like canned foods on a pantry shelf or bonds and stock certificates in a safe-deposit box. But the goods of the spirit, the supreme goods of life, cannot be treated so. Remember the man in the parable who wrapped his talent in a napkin, thinking that he could thus keep it. Though it may appeal to human weakness as a boon, there is no more debilitating doctrine than that of a "treasury of merit," and accumulation of excess virtue by saints of the past, on which sinners may now draw: a kind of spiritual dole. That the strong should help the weak, and the wise instruct the ignorant we readily agree. That is the function of the preacher and the teacher. But the help and guidance should always be given with a view to strengthening the weak, and not to perpetuate the weakness by covering it with the vicarious mantle of another's strength.

Our religion, then, is a thing which each one of us must acquire and nurture for himself. As the Scotch proverb says, "Every man must dree his own weird." But in this task we are greatly encouraged and fortified by the testimony of the past. The historical sources of ethical religion are abundant. Just when and how that tremendous event in human development took place by which man emerged from the amoral, instinctive sense-life of the animal creation to the consciousness of right and wrong, of obligation and responsibility, we do not know. Whether this consciousness was something originally implanted in man by the Creator or was discovered by man in his association with his fellows in tribe and family we may let the theologians and the anthropologists argue, as they have argued for centuries. The fact is there, and the great scholar George Romanes declared that this step into moral consciousness was the most important advance in the evolution of man. Without it he could never have appreciated progress in culture or refinement in religion. He might conceive of a god of power, surrounded as he was by the terrifying forces of nature; but to attribute to that power such moral qualities as love and mercy would have been beyond his reach.

I wonder at times whether we appreciate the abundant sources of our ethical religion with which history furnishes us; whether we realize what a tremendous stimulus to steadfastness is the sense of heirship to a great tradition. How, for example, could one preserve an unshakable faith in democracy in the face of all the perversions and betrayals of democracy one sees today, even in our own land, unless one felt the working in his own soul of something of that zeal for democracy which animated a Washington and a Lincoln? John Milton wrote, "A good book is the precious life-blood of a master-spirit, embalmed and treasured up on purpose to a life beyond life." How much more precious for life beyond life is the faith of a man who, in the midst of discouragement and defeat, can keep his eyes fixed steadily on the ideal which has inspired him: a William of Orange, who could lose every

ETHICS AS A RELIGION

battle and yet win the war against the best troops of Europe under the captains of Philip of Spain; a Washington, whom neither the sufferings of his hungry and shivering little army at Valley Forge nor the backbitings and conspiracies of his jealous critics in Congress could persuade to despair of the triumph of the cause to which he had dedicated his fortune and his sacred honor; a Lincoln, whose unflinching devotion to the task of saving the Union could blot out every thought of personal ambition or private resentment, and make him the imperishable symbol of America's destiny. Patriotism would wither without such sources to draw from. It is like a plant rooted in the soil and watered by the memories of our country's achievements. Lip service may be paid to it in oratorical exhibitions or fervent songs; but unless the *spirit* of the patriots is in the hearts of the performers all the shouting and singing will be only as sounding brass and tinkling cymbals.

So it is with religion, which is as easily counterfeited as patriotism. Not everyone who cries Lord! Lord! enters the kingdom of heaven. Our religion must be the apprehension and appropriation of eternal verities which have been the inspiration of the great prophets of righteousness in all countries and ages. No church or sect has a monopoly of these inspired ones. They belong to humanity: Plato of Athens, Jesus of Nazareth, Buddha of India, the Stoic Epictetus, the Christian St. Francis, the "God-intoxicated" Spinoza, the gloved iconoclast Emerson. Let us not ignore our heritage by neglecting the life-giving sources of our ethical religion. From all sides come voices of rebuke for the failure of men today to honor their religious heritage by earning it. Professor D. Elton Trueblood in a recent volume entitled *The Predicament of Modern Man* makes a plea for fidelity to the church as the only organ of religious edification; but he nevertheless frankly acknowledges its "tenuous hold" on its members. "The twentieth century man," he says, "is trying to live in the midst of the world storm, not as an adherent of paganism and not as an opponent of the Christian faith, but as one who adheres to that faith in the most vague and tenuous manner conceivable. He claims to be a stockholder in the Christian corporation, but the stock has been watered almost to the vanishing point and is held, moreover, by absentee owners." It is in the name of religion that we protest against this indifference to religion. It is not less religion that we want, but more religion. We see what is evident to many a serious thinker, that unless religion is divested of the irrational dogmas which still characterize the official creeds of Christendom, there is danger that it will be left as an empty formality for the conforming masses, while culture will be divorced from faith. In short, we believe that the only way to preserve a vital religion is to make it acceptable to men and women of the twentieth century.

A few years ago the Reverend James Moffatt of the Union Theological Seminary published a little book replete with learning and charming in style, entitled *The Thrill of Tradition*. It was a plea for the preservation of theology as the intellectual carrier of the religious tradition handed down through the ages. The creed, said the author, was the reasoned and systematic formulation which passed on the faith of the church from generation to generation, and without which there could be no religious community but only an incoherent mass of people lacking spiritual direction. We would agree with Dr. Moffatt on the value and vitality of a religious tradition, but we differ from him on the *kind* of religious tradition which we would have perpetuated. What we miss in his book is the recognition of the fact that religious people can "thrill" to other stimuli than the traditional theological creeds (as our Emersons and Whitmans and Adlers have proved). We also miss any discussion of the features in all the theological creeds which disqualify them from satisfying the intellectual and moral demands of man today: namely, their unverifiable assumptions, their claim to finality and their invocation of supernatural sanctions.

After the havoc of the first World War Mr. H. G. Wells interrupted his prolific output of novels to write an *Outline of History*, convinced that only a general acquaintance with the course of history could provide mankind with the knowledge necessary to prevent a world-wide collapse. He believed that the survival of civilization depended on the outcome of "the race between education and catastrophe." In the introduction to his *Outline* he wrote:

OUR ETHICAL HERITAGE

"The need for a common knowledge of the general facts of human history throughout the world has become very evident during the tragic happenings of the last few years. Swifter means of communication have brought all men closer to one another for good or evil. War becomes a universal disaster, blind and monstrously destructive. It bombs the baby in its cradle and sinks the food ships that cater to the non-combatant and the neutral. There can be no peace now, we realize, but a common peace in all the world, no prosperity but a general prosperity. But there can be no common peace and prosperity without common historical ideas. Without such ideas to hold them together in harmonious cooperation, with nothing but narrow, selfish and conflicting national traditions, races and peoples are bound to drift apart toward conflict and destruction."

If these wise words were applicable to the situation three decades ago they are doubly apposite today, when every threat to civilization that Mr. Wells mentions has enormously increased. War has become immeasurably more destructive. Narrow and selfish nationalism is more rampant. For a full generation the chronic crisis of war and the fear of war has kept the governments and people of the world on tenterhooks. The most terrible conflict in the annals of history came to an end over five years ago; yet, far from bringing the assurance of a lasting peace, the victory has assumed more and more the aspect of a troubled truce. More men are under arms today and more billions are being spent for military and naval establishments than ever before. Furthermore, while after the first World War there were sincere if futile efforts to curtail military and naval expenditures, the counsel now stressed by statesmen and generals alike is the increase and not the abatement of the armed forces. Our navy exceeds the combined navies of all the other nations of the world. We plan to keep an army of more than a million men. And meanwhile we are told that there is no possible defense against the atomic bomb. Is it not clear that the history of the last war, with its terrible climax at Hiroshima and Nagasaki, makes it necessary to rely on different means for the preservation of civilization than military force? The time for decision has come. We must shift from the battle-front of arms to the battle-front of ideals. We must meet the fanatical devotion of the totalitarians to a system which glorifies force as the only arbiter in the affairs of men by an equally firm devotion to the democratic tradition of the settlement of disputes by the give-and-take method of free discussion. And is it not also clear that for the strengthening of this process of conciliatory consultation we need all the wisdom that history can furnish, and all the encouragement supplied to us by the heroes of the past who have waged the battle of freedom against authority? For the great benefactors of the race in every age have been the few inspired seers and prophets who have had the vision of a higher worth in man and a nobler destiny for man than that recognized by the age in which they lived. This is our ethical heritage; and to feel ourselves part of this tradition of freedom, however small our part may be, must be the stimulus which gives us courage in weakness and comfort in trial, worth to our unworthiness and significance to our life.

But a challenge to our fidelity to our ethical heritage comes from those who have no faith in man's ability to shape his own destiny. The advocates of fatalism among philosophers and historians are numerous. For example, a president of the American Historical Association declared in his presidential address a few years ago that the events of history are "governed by natural laws which we must accept whether we want to or not; whose workings we cannot obviate, and which have to be reckoned with as much as the laws of gravitation and chemical affinity." The business of the historian, he continued, is to discover these laws; for "if we knew the laws of history, we might reason and act with the same intelligence and anticipation of success with which the engineers conform with the known laws of physics or the astronomers with the laws of astronomy."

Now, it is a pure assumption on the part of these fatalists that human actions are determined by inexorable laws analogous to those which govern the physical universe. It is an assumption borrowed from science in these days when science has become a veritable religion for those whose faith in a revealed religion, an inspired scripture, or an infallible church has waned. But what, after all, is this alleged law governing human actions, which is analogous to the rigid laws of physics, and which the historian is exhorted to discover in order that he may understand the past and forecast the future? Who has ever attempted to formulate such a law? Who has brought any evidence from history to prove the existence of such a law? It cannot be formulated for the simple reason that it does not exist. It is only asserted over and over again in such impressive phrases as "inevitable trends," "irresistible forces," "the wave of the future," "manifest destiny," "providence," "a divinity which shapes our ends" and the like. Gladstone spoke pontifically (as usual) of "the great social forces which move on in their weight and majesty, and which the tumult of our debates does not for a moment impede or disturb." As if it were not precisely the tumult of our debates (in which Mr. Gladstone participated freely) which set in motion all the social forces! Imagine the debates of the Constitutional Convention not affecting "for a moment" the destiny of our country! Or are our statesmen only Charlie McCarthys sitting in the lap of Fate, the great ventriloquist? Determinism in any form saps ethical idealism. It is determination that nourishes it. And there is no limit short of death to what the spirit of determination may achieve. That is the American spirit, which animated the pioneers whose persistent courage in the face of manifold dangers and hardships laid the foundations of our national inheritance, and which has inspired our public servants from George Washington to Franklin Roosevelt to build on those foundations a republic dedicated to the ethical ideal of unremitting effort. Two thousand years ago a Roman poet rebuked the idea that men must supinely accept fatalism. "Thou hast no sovereignty, O Fortune," wrote Juvenal, "if we mortals have wisdom; it is we who have called thee a goddess and placed thee in the heavens." "It is ridiculous," said our wise soldier-philosopher Mr. Justice Holmes, "to believe that we have nothing to do but to sit still and let time run over us." We must assert our faith in the power of free men to preserve a civilization in which freedom will seem to have been inevitable because we have willed that it shall persist. We need to keep in mind the good old American belief that "God helps those who help themselves." We must *make* good.

Every liberty that man enjoys has had to be fought for against inveterate opposition. In times of comparative calm we do not realize what it has cost to secure these liberties for us. It is only when they are threatened that we are keenly aware of their blessings, just as it is only when we are ill that we prize the blessings of health. Now that the world is desperately ill it behooves us to look back with gratitude to the noble company of prophets and martyrs who have labored for the emancipation of man from the fear of vengeful gods and cruel tyrants, from their own undisciplined imaginations and uncontrolled emotions. Yet how distressingly few are the people in this materialistic age who seek to know and understand these great liberators! We should be proud and honored to make their acquaintance, and they are eager to welcome us into their fellowship. But we neglect them in our pursuit of money, pleasure and social recognition. I doubt whether one out of ten of the graduates of our colleges has heard the name of Algernon Sidney or Andrew Hamilton, or read a page of John Stuart Mill or the *Federalist*. Miss Elizabeth Bentley, a former member of the Communist Party, a college graduate with a master's degree from Columbia, testified before a congressional committee in 1948 that she "grew up to womanhood without becoming acquainted with the American government." Hence, as Dorothy Thompson commented, "she was unable to discriminate between what is compatible with loyal American citizenship and what incompatible. She did not reject American democracy as, for instance, a well-trained Marxian theorist rejects it; she abandoned it without even knowing that she was doing so." What a sinister light such a case throws on our American education! And how can we expect an adequate appreciation of our heritage from people who are more interested in a spicy novel or an exciting movie than in the builders of our nation? President Eliot and Rudolph Valentino died at the same time. Reputable metropolitan newspapers devoted a few paragraphs to the greatest of American educators and filled pages with the obituary of the idol of the screen, describing how women were trampled and suffocated in the crowd which fought to get a glimpse of his face in the coffin. It's not so much the folly of these foolish "mourners" that we deplore as the fact that detailed notice of it should be taken by the press. If we allow a creeping color-blindness to moral values to obscure our vision of the heritage bequeathed to us by the great servants of human emancipation, how shall we ourselves be free to continue their work for future generations?

This struggle for human emancipation has taken place on many fronts. Most conspicuous have been its victories in politics and religion. Space does not permit of even a brief review of the steps by which tyrannies over the common man have been removed: tyrannies of mighty warlords, of feudal suzerains, of kings by divine right, of a privileged ruling class. Led by the Russells and the Sidneys in the English revolution of the seventeenth century, by the Mirabeaus and Dantons, the Washingtons and Jeffersons of the French and American revolutions of the eighteenth century, the people broke down the pretensions of arbitrary rule and vindicated the right of man as citizen to self-government. The process of religious emancipation has an even longer history, reaching back to the "dawn of conscience" in ancient Egypt. In fact the whole course of history might be summarized as a conflict between the prophet's faith in a new and better future and the priest's fidelity to a divinely sanctioned past. We of the ethical fellowship acknowledge the line of the prophets as our spiritual ancestry. To them we would pay the debt of our heritage.

But before we can pay that debt, it is obvious that we must recognize it. And here we meet with one of the saddest faults of our restless age namely, the indifference of such vast numbers of people to the sources of the liberties which they enjoy. If a man had been freed from unjust punishment by the efforts of some unknown friend, he would make every effort to discover his benefactor, and would do everything he could to repay his debt of gratitude. Now, we have all been freed by the efforts of our benefactors in the past from a worse prison than one of stone walls and iron bars: from the prison of the mind which kept men for long ages confined in the bonds of ignorance and superstition. Without the insight and courage of these benefactors we should be still imprisoned like the men in Plato's cave, with our backs to the light, and seeing on the wall in front of us only the shadows of the realities in the clear day outside. The least we can do is to acknowledge our debt to these benefactors, and spare some time from business and pleasure to make their acquaintance. In his stimulating book *Faith for Living* Lewis Mumford tells of an incident which illustrates the indifference of so many people to their spiritual heritage. "I recently asked a group of very intelligent educators," writes Mumford, "an informal series of questions to determine what share the cultivation of the inner life had in their calendar of activities. . . . How many went to church? Perhaps two out of a group of twenty. How many devoted as much as ten minutes a day to pure contemplation, free from all practical demands? None. And note, these were educators, not businessmen, almost all of them people with eight years of university education behind them." If this is a fairly typical sampling of our society, we are certainly not paying our debt to our benefactors.

We are not called upon to endure the pains and penalties which they suffered for our sakes. We are not forced to drink the hemlock or go to the stake. But let no one think that there remains no more work of liberation to be done. So long as racial hatreds drive men to persecution, so long as religious bigotry brands honest doubt as sin, so long as political hypocrisy fosters fraud and graft, so long as social snobbery despises the homespun virtues, so long as the nations prepare for war with professions of peace on their lips, so long will the task of the prophetic liberator last; so long will the road to freedom still stretch before us. "The world that we must seek," writes Bertrand Russell in his *Proposed Roads to Freedom,* "is a world in which the creative spirit is alive, in which life is an adventure full of joy and hope, based rather on the impulse to construct than upon the desire to retain what we possess or to seize what is possessed by others. It must be a world in which affection has free play, in which love is purged of the instinct for domination, in which cruelty and envy have been dispelled by happiness and the unfettered development of all the instincts that build up life and fill it with mental delights. Such a world is possible. It waits only for men to wish to create it. Meanwhile the world in which we exist has other aims. But it will pass away, burned up in the hot fire of its own passions. And from its ashes will spring a new, a younger world, full of fresh hope, with the light of morning in its eyes."

Above all, if we would-be worthy to belong to the noble company of workers for the new world of creativity and freedom, we must keep inviolate our faith in man. The path of descent to the Avemus of cynicism and despair is easy. The tentacles of a disordered past reach out to drag us down. The fogs of a distressing present close in on us to obscure the vision of the new world of our desire. We are tempted at times to cry out with Hamlet:

> *That grows to seed; things rank and gross in nature*
> *How weary, stale, flat and unprofitable*
> *Seem to me all the uses of this world!*
> *Fie on't! Ah fie! 'Tis an unweeded garden*
> *Possess it merely.*

Then let us remember the heritage of courage which we have received from those whose spirit neither disaster nor defeat could crush; whom neither kings nor priests could force to bow the head and submit to slavery of body or mind; who, when the skies seemed darkest, looked with the eye of faith beyond the clouds to the enduring sun. Let us remember that we have chosen these undaunted souls as our mentors and models, and pay our debt of gratitude to them by our utmost contribution to the unfinished task of human liberation. If humanity has never before been faced with the challenge that now confronts it, neither has it ever before had the resources, physical, intellectual and spiritual, to meet that challenge. But whether our material abundance shall be wisely used or our intellectual equipment directed toward constructive ends depends in the last analysis upon the ethical factor. That truth has been increasingly emphasized of late, not only by religious leaders but also by men in positions of political authority from the President of the United States down. The crying need of our country and the world today is for a baptism of righteousness.

> *Here in the path of every day,*
> *Here on the common human way,*
> *Is all the busy gods would take*
> *To build a heaven, to mould and make*
> *New Edens. Ours the stuff sublime*
> *To build Eternity in time.*

CHAPTER THIRTEEN

RELIGIOUS PROVINCIALISM

PROVINCIALISM may be defined as a lack of hospitality to ideas which are strange to the particular environment in which we have been brought up. It denotes a limitation in the range of our sympathies. Professor R. R. Marett, the anthropologist, tells us that when the Dutch colonists told the natives of Borneo that water in their country became so hard at certain times of the year that men and animals could walk on it, the natives refused to believe so obvious a lie. They knew that water was always liquid and never solid. Quite generally the word "provincial" is applied to the peculiar customs of speech and manners which characterize a certain geographical region, with the implication of the backwardness or crudeness of that region. In France, for example, there has always been a consciousness of the social cleft between the provinces and the capital. It is said that every professor in a provincial university looks to Paris as a Mecca. He would rather have a minor position at the Sorbonne or the College de France than be head of his department at Lyon or Lille. We had a perfect example of ingrowing provincialism in our own country at the time of the Scopes trial at Dayton, Tennessee, a generation ago. Farmer Butler, who brought the case against young Mr. Scopes for teaching evolution, was the representative of the geographical provincialism which was limited by the static customs of that mountain region. Mr. Bryan, who championed the case for the prosecution, was the representative of the psychological provincialism which refused to move out of the limitations of early evangelical indoctrination. Both were honest men according to their lights; but the lights were dim. One has only to think of the great variety in dialects, manners and social conventions among our people to realize how pervasive this trait of provincialism is. Nor is it the mark of the less educated people alone. The cultivated city dweller summering in the country is fully as provincial as the farmer's family with whom he is staying. He may be an expert on banking or railroading, but the chances are that he doesn't know the difference between a potato plant and a tomato plant. We are all likely to be ignoramuses beyond a restricted field of interests and occupations. We are all subject to Hamlet's reproof, "There are more things in heaven and earth, Horatio, than are dreamt of in your philosophy."

May I be allowed to tell of a personal experience of some sixty years ago? Immediately on being graduated from college I went out to Constantinople to teach in Robert College, founded by the missionary Cyrus Hamlin and endowed by the New York merchant Christopher Robert. It was in the days of the old crafty and cowardly Sultan Abdul Hamid II, long before the Young Turk movement under Enver and Talaat had begun the transformation of that oriental despotism into the modem republic of Kemal and Inonii. The time was the last night of the holy month of Ramadan, when Mohammedans were obliged to refrain from food and drink every day between sunrise and sunset. The place was the great mosque of Santa Sophia (the St. Peter's of Islam), which had been built by the Emperor Theodosius in the sixth century as a Christian basilica, and which, after the conquest of Constantinople in 1459, had been converted into a Mohammedan mosque. The Christian frescoes on the walls had been whitewashed over, and at the four comers of the intersection of the nave and the transept were hung huge green disks on which were engraved in golden letters texts

RELIGIOUS PROVINCIALISM

from the Koran. The scene on that holy night, as a little group of us "infidels" watched it from a balcony, was awe-inspiring. Thousands and thousands of pious Mohammedans were packed shoulder to shoulder on the floor of the mosque, and as the Moslem priest pronounced the name of Allah they fell to their knees and then forward on their faces, sending an echo through the mosque as their foreheads struck the marble floor. We looked down at the worshipers through a haze made by the smoke from the wicks of hundreds of little glass cups filled with oil and suspended from the ceiling. I thought of Milton's description of Satan's palace in hell :

From the arched roof,
Pendant by subtle magic, many a row
Of starry lamps and blazing cressets, fed
With naphtha and asphaltus.

What effect the scene had on my companions I do not know; but on me it made an indelible impression. I knew, of course, that there were other religions than Christianity; but they had always seemed remote, intangible and nonsignificant. At home I had been part of the congregation; here I was a despised infidel witnessing the fervent worship of the throng of the faithful. Never again could I regard Christianity and religion as synonymous. That phase of religious provincialism was ended.

The geneticists tell us that the individual in his evolution recapitulates the experience of the race. And history shows that the constant, if interrupted, trend of social evolution has been away from provincialism. When our remote ancestors passed the nomadic stage of hunting and fishing and with the discovery of agriculture attained a settled existence, in which they could bring their food to themselves instead of ranging far afield to find it, the first real society began. It meant the stabilizing of customs, the solidarity of tribal folkways, the fixation of ceremonials and taboos which it was death to violate. This was provincialism in its starkest form. The tribe was the ultimate determinant of social consciousness; beyond it were only enemies, outlanders, with their strange customs and gods. Then wars and migrations gradually broke down this tribal exclusiveness. Men began to learn by comparison and contrast (our only teachers) how other peoples lived. Amalgamation and adaptation followed. The Israelites, for example, to the horror of their great prophets, added the worship of the gods of the conquered Canaanites to that of their own jealous god Jehovah. The Romans imported with their captives the rites of the Egyptian Isis and the Syrian Attis, the Greek priest and the Etruscan haruspex, until the old Roman agricultural and household divinities were submerged in the elaborate pantheon of the emperors. Something like a world civilization dawned when the Pax Romana extended from Portugal to Persia and from the Scottish border to the Sahara, bringing the various nations under a common political authority and cultural influence.

But the course of history resembles a spiral rather than a straight line of advance. The Roman unity was shattered by the incursion of barbarians from the hinterlands beyond the Rhine and the Danube. The downward curve of the spiral began, which was to last through the centuries of the Dark Ages. Provincialism emerged again. Society was broken into fragments. Even the church, the successor of the empire in the task of preserving world unity ("the ghost of the empire, sitting crowned on its grave," as Thomas Hobbes called it), was not able to prevent the disintegration. Medieval feudalism was in substance a revived tribalism. The strong man built his castle on the hill, and the serfs and peasants gathered in their miserable huts in its shelter. Law and custom, industry and commerce were limited to the manor. The baron held his court "at the gate," like the lawgiver of the ancient tribe, and the litigants walked to the seat of justice. A curious term that has come down from the Middle Ages illustrates this primitive custom: namely, the "pie-powder" court, pie-powder being a corruption of the French *pied poudre*, or dusty foot. Even the horse-and-buggy days were far in the distant future.

Then the process of deprovincialization had to begin over again. The curve of the spiral commenced to rise. The Renaissance brought the humanizing influence of the ancient classical culture. Discovery and exploration widened the area of commerce and furnished the knowledge of hitherto unknown peoples. New contacts stimulated new ideas. But in this dawning of the modem age the process of social integration was not through the military conquests of a single power like Rome or the attempted dominance of the one holy Catholic Church. Instead, it was the emergence of several national states. Little by little strong kings, with the aid of the growing middle classes, triumphed over the feudal lords of provincialism. They converted the feudal levies into paid royal armies, substituted royal courts for the baronial and ecclesiastical ones, encouraged the standardization of a national language, and nurtured in their people a devotion to the nation as the symbol of their unity and the protector of their lives and property. The rise of nationalism from the fifteenth to the eighteenth century is a fascinating chapter of history. It was at the time a wholesome development, replacing anarchy by law, precariousness by security, incessant war by intervals of peace, and local systems of barter by commerce between a widening group of states. It was a slow process too, and many features of provincialism lingered until recent times. For example, at the time of the French Revolution there were four distinct languages spoken in what is the France of today. The American colonies were made into a united nation in 1776, but Thomas Jefferson five years later, in his *Notes on Virginia,* constantly speaks of his native state as "my country." And as late as 1861 Robert E. Lee, after pacing the floor of his chamber in agony for a night, decided that he must decline the offer of President Lincoln to lead the armies of the United States, and give his allegiance to the state of Virginia.

But nationalism, for all of its achievements in the age of its rise, has had its day. It has become now a new form of provincialism. The progress of science in communication and transportation has annihilated space and reduced the world to one great interdependent community in which the fortunes of every nation are bound up with those of the other nations. An isolated nationalism today is as pestiferous as the isolated feudalism of the Middle Ages. So a new chapter has opened in the history of provincialism; and the task now before the human race is to devise political and economic adjustments which will fit the increasingly intimate contacts of the nations. This is not wholly a new task. From time to time in the last few centuries men have come forward with plans for the federation of the nations, from the proposal of Henry of Navarre's minister Sully in the sixteenth century for a united Christian Europe under the leadership of France to the late Aristide Briand's "United States of Europe" and Clarence Streit's "Union Now." The Frenchman Pierre du Bois at the beginning of the eighteenth century and the German Immanuel Kant at its close proposed plans of union which might bring about universal peace. But all of these plans lacked two essential elements which must characterize the task before us today. First, they were based on the imperialistic idea of a single nation which should be predominant in the union by virtue of its wealth, prestige or military strength—an idea which is developed in Henry Luce's "The American Century." And second, they were all rather in the nature of political speculations than the response to the urgent demand of suffering peoples that the intolerable conditions of

ETHICS AS A RELIGION

devastation, starvation, slavery and war in the midst of potential plenty and security be removed. It is in the white heat of the agony of the nations that the new instruments of redemption must be forged; from

> *Iron dug from central gloom,*
> *And heated hot with burning fears,*
> *And dipt in baths of hissing tears,*
> *And battered with the shocks of doom*
> *To shape and use.*

I have intended this historical excursus on the progressive elimination of political and economic provincialism as a background for the discussion of spiritual or religious provincialism. It was Professor William Ogbum of the University of Chicago, I believe, who first used the phrase "cultural lag" to indicate the tardiness with which our social customs, educational programs and religious practices follow the rapid advance in science and technology. And the sociologist Harry Elmer Barnes has continually harped on the man who would be ashamed to drive an automobile of ancient vintage and yet entertains religious ideas which date from the Middle Ages or earlier. Why is the spiritual life of man so slow to emerge from provincialism? Perhaps one reason is that religion is so deeply rooted in the nature of man and has been so intimately connected with all his activities that it is hard for him to adjust it to changing conditions. Long before political institutions were established or scientific curiosity was aroused men had elaborate systems of religious ceremonialism. Indeed, the life of primitive man was entirely enveloped by religious prescriptions and taboos. For example, when the tribesmen went out to hunt the women were forbidden to weave, for fear that the hunter might become entangled in the threads. Men with defective teeth were not allowed to plant the corn, because then the kernels might be black and blasted. Peasant women in some parts of Europe, we are told, kept until recent times the custom of winding layer after layer of cloth around their heads like a turban, to induce the cabbages to grow big. Illustrations could be cited *ad libitum* of the persistent influence of religious trammels and taboos upon all our institutions; our schools, courts, commerce, art, music, and even our dress and diet. But one example will suffice: namely, medicine.

Medicine developed out of magic. Weird performances of the medicine man, shaking dried peas in a gourd, dancing around a patient and uttering a gibberish of incantations, were relied on to effect a cure. In the Middle Ages strange decoctions were brewed and forced down the throat of the suffering victim. What some of these alleged cures were one may read in the fascinating volume of Dr. Hans Zinsser entitled *Rats, Lice and History*. Nor did the lingering influence of magic fully disappear from medicine until fairly recent times. As late as the early eighteenth century a potency was believed to reside in the person of an anointed sovereign whose touch would heal certain diseases. King Charles II of England "touched" hundreds of persons who were waiting for him to pass by on the

ETHICS AS A RELIGION

streets of London, to be cured of scrofula, or the "king's evil," as it was called. The great Dr. Johnson remembered having been touched for the disease by Queen Anne, a portly woman in mourning for her lost children. And there are men and women today who trust to the essentially magic performance of the laying on of hands or "absent treatment" to heal them of their ills.

A second and perhaps more potent reason for the slowness with which religious ceremonialism has yielded to rational ideas has been the severity of the sanctions with which the violation of religious tradition has been punished. In primitive times it meant disaster to the tribe and death to the individual to depart from the prescribed religious routine. In the Middle Ages heresy was a worse crime than murder, because the murderer injured only the family of the victim, while the heretic spread a poison that might infect a whole people. Thus Torquemada could justify his cruelty in the Inquisition by the sophistry that to torture and burn a heretic was to do him a favor, since it might save his immortal soul from endless torture and burning. What was the physical life of a few years on earth as compared with the fate of the soul through eternity? Of course, the days of the Inquisition are past. Men are no longer burned at the stake or subjected to the thumbscrews and the rack for differing from the doctrines of the church. Yet even now we can note a lingering trace of the influence of the once terrifying sanctions against departing from the established faith. No slightest obloquy attaches to a man who investigates a scientific problem without any sense of obligation to conform to the opinions of an Aristotle, a Galen or a Ptolemy. His thought is completely free to follow every glimpse of truth that he can get. It is only in religion that the phrase "free thought" has carried with it a reproach, as if the man who confessed it were something of a social menace.

These examples of religious provincialism, so deeply rooted in the customs and so jealously guarded by the sanctions of the past, find further reinforcement in the fact that until recent times the belief prevailed that religion was a function of the state and must share the provincialism of the state. The early gods were local gods. Every city and town had its own protecting divinity, as the towns in Catholic countries today have their special saints and patrons. Moreover, the god was attached to the soil, like the serf of the Middle Ages. Cross the border to another city or state, and you left your god behind. There is an interesting illustration of this geographical aspect of religious provincialism in an Old Testament story in the second Book of Kings. Naaman was the captain of the armies of the king of Syria. But he was a leper. After a raid on one of the towns of Israel, a little girl was brought to Syria to serve as handmaiden to Naaman's wife. She said, "Would God my lord were with the prophet that is in Samaria! For he would recover him of his leprosy." Naaman went reluctantly, and when he arrived at Samaria he was bidden by the prophet Elisha to dip his body seven times in the Jordan. But Naaman was angered by this advice.[11] Are not Abana and Pharpar, rivers of Damascus, better than all the waters of Israel? May I not wash in them, and be clean?" But his servants persuaded him to follow Elisha's counsel; and when he emerged from the Jordan "his flesh came again like unto the flesh of a little child, and he was clean." So far the story is only one of the miracle myths of Elisha, like his raising of a child from the dead and causing an iron axhead to float. But now comes the interesting point to illustrate the provincialism of religion. Naaman in his gratitude vows that henceforth he will serve no other god than the God of Israel. But how can he do so in Syria? To solve the difficulty he asks for two mule loads of soil from Samaria, with which he can build an altar for the worship of Jehovah. He carries home a little bit of Israel, and the God of Israel follows the soil. Is not here the germ of the idea of holy ground still prevalent among some modem worshipers? In Pisa, Italy, is the Campo Santo, the holy burying ground for which the earth was brought from Palestine. The good Catholic must be buried in consecrated ground. Pilgrims brought home bottles of holy water from the Jordan for christening ceremonies, like Theobald Pontifex in Samuel Butler's novel *The Way of All Flesh.* One of the chief grievances against Servetus, whom Calvin had burned at Geneva, was that he had described Palestine as an arid country, whereas the Bible said that it was a land "flowing with milk and honey."

Let us ask now what are some of the unfortunate effects of religious provincialism. In the first place it tends toward an undue emphasis on formalism. The rudest and most primitive religions were almost entirely formalistic. The correct performance of prescribed rites exhausted their content. And this mere ceremonialism had the effect, as it still does for millions of people, of dulling and lulling the reason, like a kind of intellectual opiate. That is why in Russia, where the religion of the old Greek Orthodox state church was so exclusively ritualistic, Lenin could call religion "the opiate of the people." The worshiper was not encouraged to use his intellect. Education was no part of religion. Perhaps the pendulum swung too far in the opposite direction when some of the more austere sects of the Reformation repudiated every scrap of color and ceremony in their worship that would tend to take their minds off the awful duty of the individual to meet his God face to face and square his account with the great Judge on his throne. So the Puritans banished colored windows and instrumental music from their meetinghouses, John Knox declaring that the organ was "a chest of devils." So they would have no trace of ritual, Pastor John Robinson asserting that the Anglican Prayer Book "came straight out of hell." So they made the celebration of Christmas a crime and dancing around the Maypole a scandal. They gathered in their bare-walled, unheated meetinghouses (the word "church" was anathema) and sat shivering through interminable sermons, while the preacher turned and re-turned the hourglass, their souls warmed by the awful warning that most of them were destined to have warmth enough in the world to come. Samuel Morison in his *Maritime History of Massachusetts* has given as a plausible reason for the eagerness of the New England boys to get away to see the desire to escape the tedious Puritan sermons.

Another effect of religious provincialism is its tendency to oppose the new insights and fresh discoveries of the eternally curious mind of man. Such opposition has been most conspicuous in the field of science. Having accepted as divinely inspired Scripture a collection of books written centuries before the truths revealed by science were dreamed of, orthodox theologians have consistently obstructed the spread of scientific knowledge from Copernicus to Darwin. With few exceptions, like the Austrian priest Mendel with his biological experiments, ecclesiastics have made no contribution whatever to science. It was not until well into the nineteenth century that the Catholic Church gave up its lingering opposition to the Copernican system of astronomy; and, as the Scopes trial proved, there are still people who believe that the acceptance of the doctrine of evolution means the surrender of religion. In short, owing to its religious provincialism, Biblical Christianity has sought to draw a curtain over the inquiring mind. "Don't reason; believe!" cried St. Bernard in his controversy with Abelard, that heretical *enfant terrible* of the twelfth century, who retorted, "How can I believe what I cannot understand?" To seek to understand was in St. Bernard's opinion a mark of contumacy and rebellion. As one historian has put it in speaking of the Puritans, "Their windows were open toward Jerusalem, but closed to every other point of the compass."

Closely related to this intellectual obscurantism is a certain smugness which is likely to characterize religious provincialism. It is like the geographical provincialism which finds it hard to understand the feelings and customs of people who live in another part of the country. "My gracious," said a woman who lived in the mountain region of Kentucky to a man who came from New York, "it must make you feel queer to live so far away." How reluctant the victims of religious provincialism have been to appreciate other types of excellence than those with which they are immediately familiar! The Hebraic-Christian tradition, for example, has been so dominant in the Western world for centuries that it has been accepted as synonymous with religion itself. Matthew Arnold, that "reluctant Christian," tried to redress the balance by pointing out in his volume of *Hebraism and Hellenism* the contributions which the Greeks had made to our culture. And beyond this lie the philosophies and religions of the East, rich in ethical instruction. One might think John Calvin's kind of exclusive religious provincialism outgrown today. But one reads in a book by Herbert Hoover and Hugh Gibson on *The Problems of Lasting Peace* the following statement: "Christianity has been unique among religious faiths in its preaching of peace and compassion." What misinformation, what smugness! Do the authors know nothing of the preaching of peace and compassion by the Buddha or Confucius, the Bahaist or the Hindu? Or perhaps do they consider such outlandish religions unworthy of notice? And what a temptation to moral smugness is the conviction that one belongs to the "elect." Think of the intolerable behavior of the elect in Puritan New England, those pompous, humorless busybodies who went about nosing into the private lives of the community, disciplining the magistrates, discovering and executing witches, exiling dissidents from the colony, and generally "throwing their weight about" as agents commissioned by divine will to keep the people obedient to their own narrow interpretation of religion.

The most serious of all the effects of religious provincialism, however, is the temptation to persecution. We need not dwell on the religious wars of the past which have stained the pages of history with blood: the atrocities of the Duke of Alba's troops in the Netherlands, the massacre of the Huguenots on St. Bartholomew's Eve, Cromwell's slaughter of the Catholics at Drogheda. Those things are over. The growing spirit of humanity forbids men any longer to torture and kill their fellows for celebrating the mass or holding up two fingers instead of three in the sign of baptism. Yet in a milder way the subtle forms of persecution have by no means been eradicated from our society. Whenever men believe that they have a truth which is fixed and final by divine authority, the more earnest their conviction, the more likely they will be to view with disapproval those who do not share that belief, and the more tempted they will be to use some measure of compulsion in pressing that belief. They may even deceive themselves into thinking that they are entirely free from any spirit of coercion, as a certain Catholic professor at the Sorbonne did when he replied to Alfred Fouillée, "Neither today nor ever in its history has the Catholic Church presumed to impose its doctrines on anybody by force." And this in the face of the dismal record of persecution by Catholic and Protestant alike in the pages of history! The simple truth is that dogmatic religion, which is always a manifestation of spiritual provincialism, leads straight to intolerance, and that intolerance is the matrix of persecution. That today committees composed of Catholics, Protestants and Jews are meeting to emphasize the common elements which can unite them in brotherhood is a testimony to the kindly irenic spirit of these gentlemen. We must applaud their good will. But at the same time we cannot escape the conviction that there is no ground of real unity possible so long as they hold to the traditional dogmas of their sects. At best it will be a tacit agreement to soft-pedal the dogmas. Will the good Catholic surrender the official doctrine of the infallibility of the pope, or the good Protestant accept it? Will the orthodox Protestant abandon his faith in the deity of Christ, or the pious Jew embrace that faith? These are not rhetorical questions, nor are they captious or irrelevant. They go to the very heart of the matter. So long as the provincialism of the creeds, which by their very nature are separative, retains its hold on men, the hope of a religion of universal brotherhood is an illusion.

In its present anguish the world is looking forward as never before to the elimination of the political and economic provincialism which has set state against state and class against class. It will be a slow process, as we all realize. But unless that end is courageously pursued we have nothing to expect but the endless recurrence of war. And since a human personality in its highest development is not a hodgepodge of conflicting ideas and desires, but an integrated and balanced whole, it is impossible for the universalization of political and economic concepts to proceed unless there is a corresponding widening of our spiritual vision. The doctrines embalmed in the official confessions of the various churches, and still preached from their pulpits, albeit with diminishing conviction, no longer fit the spiritual needs of men. They are cramping and confining. Even Christianity itself, superior as it undoubtedly is to many other of the religions of the world, is too narrow a framework for what Professor John Dewey has called "a common faith." The need of today is for a truly universal religion, one which is divested of all the trappings of inherited theologies and ceremonies, one which can appeal on purely ethical grounds to the aspirations of earnest souls of every race, color and clime for deliverance from evil and attainment of inward peace.

CHAPTER FOURTEEN

THE TIMELINESS
OF ETHICAL RELIGION

I N THE YEAR 1582 a tract was published in Middelburg, Holland, with the title *On Reformation Without Tarrying for Anie.* It was written by Robert Browne, an Englishman who was spending his second year in exile from his native land because of his heretical religious views. Copies of this and other writings of Browne were

ETHICS AS A RELIGION

smuggled into England, and two of his followers were executed by the Elizabethan magistrates for circulating them. It was a time of great religious ferment in Europe. The Reformation inaugurated by Martin Luther a half a century earlier, and carried on by Zwingli, Calvin, Knox, Melanchthon and others, had torn large sections of Europe away from the papal authority, and a succession of bloody religious wars between Catholics and Protestants filled the second half of the sixteenth century. They were raging in France when Browne wrote, while across the Channel Queen Elizabeth, herself following the Catholic rites in her private worship, was supporting the Protestant cause as a good patriot in the struggle against King Philip of Spain, who was attempting to win England back to the Catholic fold. The defeat of the Spanish Armada came six years after the publication of Browne's tract. It meant the definitive severance of England from Rome.

But the Elizabethan tolerance did not extend to the religious independents or "separatists," who were originally called Brownists. Her Act of Uniformity required strict adherence to the ceremonies of the Anglican Church as elaborated by her father, Henry VIII—the wearing of the surplice, the presence of the altar, auricular confession, the use of the Prayer Book—all of which were abhorrent to the separatists as vestiges of "popery." They were convinced that no real religious reformation could be looked for from the bishops and magistrates. "Come out from among them and be ye separate," was their text. The time was ripe for decision. They should obey their conscience without tarrying for any lead from the clergy or fearing any persecution from the state. So they were "clapped up in prison" and driven into exile. Elizabeth's successor, James I, declared that he would make them conform or harry them put of the land.

The argument of Robert Browne's pamphlet, liberally sprinkled with texts from the Old and the New Testaments, was that the civil authorities had no right to prescribe forms of belief and worship for the individual Christian or to punish him for his religious nonconformity, provided his conduct did not offend the civil law. This sensible position, so generally recognized today as to seem axiomatic, was regarded in the sixteenth century as a most dangerous innovation and a menace both to the purity of religion and to the authority of government. If every Tom, Dick and Harry were allowed to choose his own religion, it would not be long before he would be claiming a voice in the government, said the same King James, with a prophetic insight which one would not expect from that monarch's dull and obstinate mind. "No bishop, no king," was his slogan. It took many years of struggle before Robert Browne's doctrine of the release of religion from the dominance of ecclesiastical and civil authorities was sanctioned by public opinion. Browne's disciple, Roger Williams, brought the doctrine to Massachusetts in the seventeenth century, and was driven into exile in the depths of a New England winter for preaching it. Thomas Jefferson, in the eighteenth century, fought for a decade to have it incorporated into the laws of Virginia, and regarded the separation of church and state in that colony as a service to his country of equal importance with the writing of the Declaration of Independence and the founding of the University of Virginia. For Browne it was not enough to repudiate the pope and the councils, as Luther had done, nor to inveigh against vestments, organs and altars with John Knox. All the reformers of the sixteenth century had left their work half finished. They had abandoned one authority only to substitute another: the princes, the bishops, the synods, the presbyteries. But Browne carried the spirit of the Reformation to its logical conclusion in the freedom of the individual from *every* external religious authority. He is the father of our Roger Williamses and Thomas Jeffersons and all the other aposdes of religious liberty. And he deserves to be remembered and honored today as a major prophet of human emancipation.

I have taken Robert Browne's quaint title as the point of departure for the discussion of the present need for religious reformation "without tarrying for any." Our times are very different from his; our problems are not the same. But the pressure is upon us now, as never before within the memory of men, to adapt our religious beliefs and practices to the scientific, psychological and humanistic "climate of opinion" of the present age. The provincial and parochial concepts of religion which satisfied our fathers are no longer acceptable to us. In the religious as in the political world we are living in an age of chronic crisis, "between two worlds, one dead, the other

THE TIMELINESS OF ETHICAL RELIGION

waiting to be born." Multitudes of people in confusion of spirit are seeking for a religion which will enlist their reverence without at the same time offending their common sense. They are emancipated from the fear of hellfire; they have ceased to believe in miracles; they are no longer awed by the claims of a priesthood of any denomination to be the mediators of a divine revelation; they know that there is no such thing as an expert in religion, like an expert in engineering or chemistry, and that no donning of ecclesiastical vestments or handling of allegedly holy objects can make such an expert. For religion is the greatest of levelers. We are all together in this world of joy and sorrow: Jew and Gentile, rich and poor, exalted and humble, learned and simple, seeking not to penetrate the impenetrable mysteries over which the theologians of the past have spent their mental energies, but to find a religion which will release our latent moral energies and give direction, purpose, poise and meaning to our lives. This is not the task of any consecrated clergy alone. It is our common social duty. Wherever and whenever any member of the human family makes his contribution to this fund of moral idealism he is thereby a true minister of religion. Why do we tarry for any? The word is nigh us, even in our hearts:

The word we had not sense to say,
Who knows how grandly it had rung?

Let us examine some of the reasons which deter us from a more courageous and forthright proclamation of our ethical faith. In the first place there is the argument addressed to humility. Is it not presumptuous to question the truth of doctrines which have been believed for centuries by men of unquestioned learning and character, and to which millions give their allegiance today? Who are we to set up our opinions against the long tradition of orthodox Christianity?

The popular slogan, "Fifty million people can't be wrong," is a specious argument from every point of view. Neither the antiquity of a doctrine nor the prevalence of it is any proof of its truth. The history of the emergence of such measure of truth as we have attained in every field of scientific and philosophical investigation testifies to the same obstructive tactics on the part of organized religion, in the name of safeguarding traditional beliefs. It is so much easier and more comfortable to believe than it is to think. But a little serious thought should convince us that the antiquity of a belief, far from being a reason for its truth, is likely to be a camouflage for its error. And as for the argument from numbers, it is only necessary to reflect that not a single reform in politics, economics, education, or any other department of human endeavor has come from the majority. Their motto has always been, "What was good enough for my father is good enough for me." Religion is no exception to this rule. Indeed, it is the chief illustration of it.

It is obvious that if the specious arguments from antiquity and numbers as the guarantees of truth were allowed to prevail, there could be no progress in the world. We

THE TIMELINESS OF ETHICAL RELIGION

should be condemned to a stagnant civilization, which means a decaying civilization. It is the courageous innovators who, generally at the cost of obloquy and persecution, have provided the ozone of reform which keeps the world from suffocation in the exhausted air of tradition.

Count me o'er earth's chosen heroes, they were souls who stood alone,
While the men they agonized for hurled the contumelious stone.

There would have been no United States of America if the patriots of 1776 had been satisfied with the political status of their fathers, and if George Washington had heeded the warning of the Tory clergyman Boucher not to lift his hand against his anointed king. There would have been no Christianity if Jesus had found the religion of his father "good enough" for him. He was a great religious innovator, a rebel against the petrified ordinances of the Jewish temple and synagogue, scandalizing the zealots by breaking the Sabbath laws, treating the despised Samaritan like a brother, mingling with publicans and sinners. He was always ready to forgive the erring. His rare outbursts of denunciation were reserved for the self-righteous scribes and Pharisees, the hypocrites who washed the outside of the cup and tithed their mint and cummin, the whited sepulchers of orthodoxy. And for this defiance of the current religion he was handed over to the Roman authorities to be crucified on a trumped-up charge of treason.

ETHICS AS A RELIGION

No, the courageous fidelity to conviction is not presumptuousness. It is a duty the neglect of which, for any consideration of the antiquity or the prevalence of doctrines which do not enlist our honest support, is a sign of moral cowardice. We must be the architects and builders of our own religious faith, with, of course, the humble recognition of all that the faith of other seekers in other ages has to teach us. The decision comes down to the individual conscience. I like that saying of the Indian Dhammapada, "By one's self is evil done, and by one's self is one purified." Or in Emerson's modem version, "Trust thyself; every heart vibrates to that iron string." We do not feel obliged to assent to or apologize for systems of philosophy or theories of science devised by ancient thinkers according to their lights. Why should it be different with systems of religion? Men of today are infinitely better qualified to write a confession of faith than were the Westminster divines of the seventeenth century or the papal delegates to the Council of Trent. Why should we let their truth be "our jailer," as Lowell asked? Why should we tarry in the religious reformation which we believe is due, because of creeds weighted with old sanctions or ceremonies performed by large numbers? It seems to me not humility but treason to faith in the potentialities of man to contend that he must rely for spiritual development on some authority external, traditional and supernatural. In a recent book entitled *Christianity in Peril* the Reverend Andrew R. Osbom writes: "Where is good to get its dynamic power? Dynamic evil

THE TIMELINESS OF ETHICAL RELIGION

springs from selfish desire with its underlying animal urges. Good must derive its force from a higher power. . . . But if in the last analysis it is found that this power is no more than an association of human beings motivated by good will, it seems highly doubtful if it will possess the moral drive necessary for the task." Here is the crux of the whole matter. Here is the old leaven of orthodoxy working in Mr. Osborn's mind: namely, the corruption of man through Adam's fall. Human dynamic is sufficient to account for evil, but there is no human dynamic sufficient to produce good. The mere "association of human beings motivated by good will" is not enough. Supernatural power must be called in, and so the way is opened which leads logically to the Calvinistic doctrine of the absolute will of God and the consequent degradation of man. If the dynamic of good is not to be found in human beings, then it is vain to look for it elsewhere. For all the "good" we know or man can conceive is what Kant called the absolute good—the good will.

We may dismiss, then, as invalid the argument that we should tarry in our effort for religious reform out of a respect for the antiquity or the prevalence of inherited doctrines. Their antiquity is no proof of their truth, and their prevalence is more a matter of appearance than of fact. As long ago as the seventh century a bishop of Seville declared that the Roman Catholic faith was believed "always, everywhere and by everybody" (*semper, ubique et ab omnibus*). The claim was false then, and such a claim for any religion is false now. As a matter of historical fact, there never has been a time when dissenters have not abounded, and it is due to them that religion has been progressively purged of its irrelevant and irrational elements. The task is not finished. At this time of world crisis, when we are challenged as never before to vindicate our faith in political, economic and educational liberty, religion too must be freed from the inconsistencies of creed and the formalities of worship which fail to strengthen our spiritual life. We are on the "religious frontier," to use Percival Chubb's apt phrase. Many even of those men and women who are still nominally connected with the various churches are psychologically crossing that frontier into the no man's land of religious indifference, doubt or despair. Can we not arrest them with a religion which will at once satisfy their minds by the elimination of incomprehensible dogmas and fortify their hearts by its appeal to the ethical potentialities which are latent in every human being? At the beginning of the Christian era the basilicas, or law courts of Rome, were converted into churches. What a revival of true religion we would have today if the churches were converted into centers of instruction and exhortation for the propaganda of ethics!

A second argument often used as a deterrent from religious reform without tarrying for any is the appeal to loyalty. Will you abandon the faith of your father or mother or the religious teaching you received in the tender years of childhood? At first sight this argument, like the one for humility, seems to have validity. But honest thinking will, I think, convince one of its speciousness. In the first place,

THE TIMELINESS OF ETHICAL RELIGION

the religion of one's father or mother may have been only the acceptance of a tradition handed down by their father or mother, and so on back for generations. And even if the religion of father or mother was a burning personal conviction, no worthy father or mother would wish a son or daughter to accept it if it were not equally convincing to them. Filial respect and love need in no wise be impaired by a difference in religious belief. If a dour old Scotch Presbyterian disinherited his son or drove his daughter from his door because they rejected Calvinism, it was not his religion but his cussedness that prompted the act. There is a loyalty to truth which transcends any loyalty to persons. We cannot choose what we believe in order to please or placate anyone. For we believe what we must believe from the weight of evidence presented to the mind. Was it not this inescapable obligation which Jesus spoke of when he said, "He that loveth father or mother more than me is not worthy of me." It was not a personal allegiance that he asked for, but loyalty to the truth of his message. And no religious teacher is worthy of the name who values a personal following above fidelity to the message with which he feels himself to be entrusted. Parents no doubt do wisely in instructing their children in what they believe to be religious truth. No one ought ever to regret such training. Perhaps the young Jesus was taught the rabbinical lore of his time. At any rate, the story in the Gospels is that he was found at an early age disputing with the doctors in the temple. But when he had arrived at years of maturity he left the temple and declared that its ceremonies were superseded by a "new Commandment," the law of love. Was this new loyalty inconsistent with his respect and affection for his mother? Did it lessen his love for her as he looked down on her from the cross? There is one loyalty that is supreme, and that loyalty is to the dictates of conscience. The man who violates that finds all other loyalties infected with the germ of disloyalty. He is like the knight Lancelot in the *Idylls of the King,* who tried to remain loyal to himself and at the same time to his guilty love for Queen Guinevere:

> *His honor rooted in dishonor stood,*
> *And faith unfaithful kept him falsely true.*

"Faith unfaithful" is a phrase which might well be used to characterize loyalty to a person which conflicts with the supreme loyalty to one's ideal.

> *This above all: to thine own self be true,*
> *And it must follow as the night the day,*
> *Thou canst not then be false to any man.*

There is a third argument raised against the courageous pursuit of religious reform. It is the appeal to sympathy; and, like the appeals to humility and loyalty, it too seems at first sight to have much validity. It is expressed by Tennyson in his familiar lines in "In Memoriam":

> *Leave thou thy sister when she prays*
> *Her early heaven, her happy views;*
> *Nor thou with shadowed hint confuse*
> *A life that leads melodious days.*

THE TIMELINESS OF ETHICAL RELIGION

Now certainly our aim is not to go about robbing sisters of their faith, but rather to recommend a faith to those who are already "confused" which we believe to be more invigorating than the one they have and more helpful still to a life of "melodious days." If any prefer to retain their "early heaven," they surely have a right to do so; but we are not therefore obliged to conceal our own faith for fear of "confusing" them. An orthodox lady once said to a friend of mine, "Take care that you do not offend me by expressing your radical religious opinions." To which he replied, "Madam, have you ever thought that you might offend *me* by expressing your orthodox opinions?" St. Paul has a passage in his first letter to the Corinthians in which he seems to me to present a mistaken and rather sentimental idea of sympathy. He is speaking of the liberty of a Christian, especially in regard to the eating of the meat of animals killed in sacrifices; and he says truly that it makes one neither better nor worse to eat such meat. But then he goes on to say, "But take heed lest by any means this liberty of yours become a stumbling block to them that are weak. . . . Wherefore if meat make my brother to offend, I will eat no flesh while the world standeth." The answer to such an argument is that the weaker brother has no right to be offended if I eat meat. And if he persists in being offended he may become a bully to his neighbor. In my youth I heard the evangelist Dwight L. Moody preach a sermon in which he likened free-thinkers to men who go about deliberately knocking the crutches out from under cripples. Mr. Moody, believing in the fall of Adam and the consequent utter sinfulness of man, naturally regarded all men as cripples needing the crutches of dogma to lean upon. He was neither shocked nor dismayed by this debased view of man, but thought it the plan of God himself from all eternity. We do not hold this view. We know that we err and come short of the ideals which we strive to attain. We need no evangelist to tell us of our failings. But we do not believe that we are a race of cripples needing to go on crutches all our lives. Far from seeking to knock the crutches out from under men, we are striving to help them throw away their crutches and stand on their own feet. "By one's self is evil done; by one's self is one purified." We cannot therefore allow the argument of sympathy for the "weaker brother" to deter us from following the path of religious reform which our conscience dictates, any more than we can "tarry" because one says that we are presumptuous to question beliefs which have the sanction of antiquity and the support of multitudes, or because another says that we show disloyalty to parents or teachers in outgrowing the beliefs which they have handed down to us. Our responsibility in the matter of conscience is individual and inescapable. We must follow the truth as we see it, no matter who commands or reproves, who is pleased or offended. For the only way to fuller truth is through the truth we know today.

There are other influences than these which we have analyzed that tempt us to tarry on the way to religious reform. There is the constant solicitation of material interests to absorb our attention and divert our thought from the greatest of all concerns, Our spiritual well-being. Inertia and moral indifference impair the alertness of the will to good. A bent toward fatalism and the idea of "the wave of the future" causes many to drift with the tide of custom and conformity instead of stemming it when it turns into channels of evil.

And now, having examined some of the reasons which cause men to tarry in religious reform, let us conclude on the more positive note of the inspiration which bids us not to tarry. For we believe that our ethical faith is founded on obedience to a universal law. This statement needs some explanation. "Law" is a word which has various meanings. There is first a law of the world of nature. The Greeks, who have given us most of our scientific and philosophical terms, called the law *physis,* which we translate as "nature." It is a law entirely independent of human agency. We do not make, but discover, the laws of nature. They have existed from all time. The law of gravitation, for example, was just as valid before Newton deduced its operation from the falling apple as it is now. The ancient cave man recognized that it would work when he dug a pit and concealed it with branches in order to trap an elephant. We realize the futility of any attempt to break or alter the laws of nature, and we smile at the efforts of primitive men to do so. An eclipse of the sun cannot be stopped by magic rites or a pestilence halted by prayer. Obedience to these natural laws involves no moral choice or responsibility. It is only a matter of plain common sense. Obviously, then, it is not this impersonal and inexorable law of nature which we mean when we say that our ethical faith is founded on obedience to law.

A second kind of law is entirely man-made. It consists both of statutes enacted by lawgivers or orders decreed by rulers, and somewhat more vaguely of customs which have come to be recognized as binding. In contrast to the physical laws of nature, man-made laws can be broken, and it is their infraction which gives business to the profession of the law. So accustomed are we to thinking of law as this mass of legislation and custom by which the behavior of society is governed that we confine the word "lawyer" to the man who deals with it, and never think of calling a physicist or an astronomer a lawyer, although he is dealing with laws just as truly as the lawyer is. Again, it is not this law of the statute books that is the basis of our ethical inspiration, though as good citizens we intend to obey the law, even though it may seem to us ill-advised, like the prohibition law, for example. Abraham Lincoln, in spite of his abhorrence of slavery, declared that he would obey the iniquitous Fugitive Slave Act of 1850 so long as it stood on the statute books. Occasionally the problem is presented of moral responsibility for resistance to these man-made laws, and in those rare cases the duty to conscience may overrule obedience to the law. The rebel will then say with St. Paul and Emerson, "We ought to obey God rather than man." No lover of liberty would condemn the philanthropists who helped fugitive slaves to escape to freedom by the underground railroad.

THE TIMELINESS OF ETHICAL RELIGION

Now, besides the inexorable physical law of nature and the man-made law of statute and custom, there is a third kind of law which transcends both in majesty. This is the spiritual law. The Greeks called it *melos,* from which our word "melody" is derived. It was an eternal thing, "not born of yesterday or today," as the maiden Antigone replied to King Creon when she defied him by performing the burial rites for her dead brother. Plato is never wearied of praising this law of melody, which constitutes the harmony of the spheres and is the sum and substance of all good. When a man is in tune with this law his life is harmonious and melodic. But to rise to the conception of this law a man must have faith. He must believe that the universe is friendly, and that his own striving to attain the good, the beautiful and the true brings a partial but increasing insight into the absolute truth of which he has glimpses in his moments of inspiration. Obedience to this spiritual law is not a matter of compulsion, as in the case of the physical laws, nor is it a matter of conformity, as in the case of the man-made laws; rather is it an act of faith, an affirmation growing out of our experience of peace and poise even in the midst of conflict and sorrow. And it is obedience to this melodic law on which our ethical faith is founded.

The objection is often raised that there can be no sure basis of ethics because morals are relative. What is considered moral in one age or in one part of the world becomes immoral at other times or in other places. But this acknowledged relativity of morals which disturbs so many good people is no argument at all against the constant validity of ethics. Ethics stands on a higher plane than morals. My old teacher of philosophy, Professor George Palmer, used to say, "Ethics is related to morals as geometry is to carpentry." Ethics is the science of the right, while morals is the application of the science. The carpenter must know the properties of the square, the circle and the angle before he can construct his work. And the properties never change, however good or bad the work may turn out. We could put the matter in another form of comparison, adapted to our discussion of the different kinds of law. Morals aims at obedience to *lex* and *nomos,* the law of statute and custom. Ethics, on the other hand, is concerned with obedience to *melos,* the law of harmony in the universe and in our own hearts. If our ethical faith is unwavering, the morals will take care of themselves. Men do not gather grapes of thorns or figs of thistles.

It is then the compulsion of this spiritual law of inward harmony that urges us to seek ethical perfection. The materially minded may scoff at it as a figment of an impractical brain. Religion, said the old philosopher Heraclitus, is a "sacred disease." Lenin called it "the opium of the people." And a cynic of our day writes, "The rich want power and the poor want ham and eggs." But we know that such a debasing philosophy of life is false. Neither rich nor poor can live by bread alone. Jeremiah, perhaps the greatest of the Hebrew prophets, languished in a dungeon because he dared to proclaim the infidelity of Israel to the ethical demands of their God. "I will put

THE TIMELINESS OF ETHICAL RELIGION

my law in their inward parts, and in their hearts will I write it." Jesus declared that it profited a man nothing if he gained the whole world and lost his own soul. No, our ethical faith is not something salvaged from a foundered creed. It is a present and living conviction of the deepest need of man, the need to recognize and obey that inward law of righteousness which brings him into tune with the harmony of the spheres and makes him brother to all the noble souls that have labored, often in sorrow and anguish, to win the world to faith in the eternal reality of the spiritual law: Jeremiah in his dungeon, Jesus in the shadow of the cross, the martyr facing wild beasts in the arena, the heretic burned at the stake, the dissenter from the sanctioned creed driven into exile. These brave souls did not tarry for any in testifying to the faith that was in them. Few of us have their sublime courage. Nor in these days of larger tolerance is religious dissent (at least in our favored land) punished with persecution or exile. We should, then, be the more willing to testify bravely to our ethical faith, in the face of any social disapproval or misunderstanding that we may meet. In obedience to the supreme law of righteousness we should follow the dictates of conscience "without tarrying for any." We should take for our motto that word of Seneca's pilot: "O Neptune, you may sink or save my bark; but I will keep the rudder true."

CHAPTER FIFTEEN

ENDURING VALUES IN RELIGION

RELIGION is the most important factor in a man's life. Yet it is the least often discussed or referred to in his diverse social and personal relations. When Gilbert Chesterton remarked that a man's religion was the most important thing to know about him, George Bernard Shaw replied that a man's religion was precisely the thing we knew least about him. Ministers, priests and rabbis preach their sermons and perform their rituals week after week, and the members of the congregation leave church or synagogue with a sense of spiritual benefit received or duty done, to go their way to the various pursuits which absorb their attention for the next six days. They discuss politics, the high cost of living, the prospects of peace or war, the latest best seller, the merits of television or what not, but keep whatever thoughts they have about religion to themselves. This reticence may be due to a feeling that religion is too sacred a thing to talk about, or that it is a subject reserved for the clergy, or that it is of too little practical importance to warrant discussion. Here then is the strange paradox of what is most important in a man's life receiving less consideration in his daily contacts than his business prospects, his professional duties or even his social ambitions.

Despite this apparent conspiracy of silence on the subject of religion, we have abundant evidence that no other subject has so constantly and persistently appealed to the intellect and the emotions of man. Anthropologists tell us that even among the most primitive peoples they have never found a tribe without some form of religion, whether it consisted in ascribing a mystic power to a stone, a tree or a spring, or in bowing down to a graven image fabricated by their own hands. And from these crudest manifestations of religion men have advanced through their discovery of the laws of nature and the progressive refinement of their manners and morals to conceptions of religion in which God is the symbol for the highest aspirations of their own lives. He is still, and for us mortals must ever be, the embodiment of a human ideal. Furthermore, we testify in a quite unreflecting way to the transcendent place of religion in life when we use such expressions as "business is his religion" or "Communism is his religion."

Now, in attempting to discover the enduring values in religion we must be on our guard against confusing the mere persistence of the forms and ceremonies of religion with their inherent value. For in no other field than religion has there been so determined a reluctance to abandon traditional dogmas in the light of increasing knowledge. Of course, in the days of comparative ignorance men accepted dogmatic and often fantastic theories to satisfy their curiosity in regard to other matters than religion. Medieval maps, for example, show what queer ideas of geography they had before the voyages of Columbus, Magellan and Vespucius revealed the shape and size of the earth and the relative position of its lands and oceans. Medieval medicine was a mixture of mythology and miracle. Cures were expected from draughts of potions in which ground bones had been mixed with stag's blood, or from draining from the patient's body what was believed to be his own poisoned blood. George Washington's death in 1799 was hastened if not caused by the copious bloodletting resorted to by his physicians. And what a role the astrologers have played with their casting of horoscopes and their mythological psychology assigning jovial, mercurial or saturnine characters to men according to the dominant influence of the planets at their birth. But all these strange answers to man's questionings about physical phenomena have been relegated to the category of superstition—a word which means literally unprofitable survivals. They no longer occupy our attention except as historical fossils, showing the stages of ignorance through which the race has passed. If the same cannot be said of religious dogmas, if millions of people still hold to beliefs or professions of belief which are incompatible with reason, the explanation lies, I think, in the fact that the religious dogmas have not been held as hypotheses, subject to modification in the light of advancing knowledge (like the once-held views on geography or medicine), but have claimed a supernatural sanction for their lasting and unchanging validity. The very fact that the word "superstition" is now applied almost exclusively to religion is proof that it is in this field that the survival of unprofitable ideas is to be found.

There are some who argue that religion has no value at all. I once had a neighbor, a learned, upright and genial man, who used to say that the twin curses of the world were religion and patriotism. The latter puffed people up with boastful pride, disguised under the name of national honor, and from generation to generation had set nation against nation in wars which drenched the world in blood. If patriotism was not, in Dr. Johnson's phrase, "the last refuge of scoundrels," it was, he maintained, the chief arsenal of the warmonger. And religion was worse than

Lenin's "opiate of the people." It was a virus of intolerance injected into the zealot's veins. Now, it is unfortunately true that crimes have been committed in the name of patriotism and religion, as Madame Roland on her way to the guillotine deplored the crimes committed in the name of liberty. The frenzied crowds in the squares of Rome shouting, *"Duce! Duce!"*; the starry-eyed German women breathing the words *"unser Fiihrer"* in hushed and reverential voices, believed that they were the patriots of patriots. And the men who heaped the fagots around the stake of Joan of Arc and rang the bells in celebration of the Massacre of St. Bartholomew had no doubt that they were serving the will of God and the welfare of his church. *"Corruptio optimi pessima!"*—the corruption of the best is the worst. It is not patriotism that moves a nation to despise, provoke and attack its neighbor, but the horrid caricature of patriotism, which is chauvinism. It is not religion that urges men to intolerance and persecution, but the shabby substitute for religion that furnishes a zeal for hate but fails to inspire the virtue of love.

We are seeking to define the *enduring* values of religion; and that phrase implies that there have been and are values attributed to religion which are fugitive and insubstantial values. To catalogue such attributed values would be to write the history of religion from the days when the savage set his fabricated idol on a rock or a hill and made to it the obeisance which would protect him from his foe. For the people of the Greco-Roman world the value of religion lay in the contract by which the gods were bound to requite with supernatural aid the ceremonies and sacrifices properly performed by the state or the family. "If I have built a shrine acceptable to thee, O Apollo," prays the priest in Homer, "send now thine arrows of destruction upon the Argive host." The ancient Hebrew found the value of religion in the promise that Jehovah would eventually, through the saving remnant of his people, bring all the nations of the earth to the holy hill of Zion. For the early Christians religion meant the assurance of a heavenly crown if they endured to the end in faith in the risen Lord and triumphed over the persecutions of the pagans and the temptations of the flesh. Theologians from Thomas Aquinas to President Patton of Princeton have valued religion as a system of revealed doctrines which were to be made intelligible to men by the processes of logic; while the mystics dismissed reasoning and sought religious peace in the absorption of their being in the infinite perfection of God.

Doubtless some traces of all these types of value persist in the consciousness of the seeker for religious satisfaction today. Men still pray to a heavenly power to ward off harm and reward virtue. Men still hope for an eternal life beyond the grave. The old Hebrew dream of the gathering of all the nations of the earth to the holy hill of Zion finds its Christian counterpart in the efforts of the missionaries to spread the Gospel until "earth's remotest nations have heard Messiah's name." And the mystic sense of being one with the power that moves the sun and stars brings strength and comfort to many a troubled heart. Let no one despise the religious values which have made his neighbor's life more tolerable and purposeful. For we are all embarked together on the voyage of life whose desired haven is still shrouded in the mists of mortal ignorance and sin. Religion must be our guide and compass. And each one of us must search his soul for the enduring values in religion which give purpose and consistency to his own brief life.

However, we meet with several alleged values in religion which, instead of ennobling life, tend to debase it. Chief among these is fear. For uncounted numbers of people religion means the confession of such doctrines and the performance of such ceremonies as will enable them to escape the eternal punishment prescribed for those who have not been redeemed by the grace of God. But fear of punishment as a deterrent of wrongdoing adds nothing to one's moral stature. On the contrary, it tempts one to resort to such substitutes for self-discipline as casuistry and self-exculpation to escape the threatened punishment. Nor is the often urged view that the value of religion consists in the restraint which it imposes on those elements of society who would indulge in deliberate evil except for the fear of punishment, a view that we can accept as conducive to moral growth. All through the ages men have had an awful presentiment that divine retribution waited upon evil-doing. Long before the advent of Christianity, which intensified the fear by the picture of the eternal torment which awaited the unbeliever, the ancient pagan writers had dwelt on the theme of divine nemesis. Aeschylus, the most religious-minded of the Greek dramatists, wrote in the chorus of the *Eumenides:* "It is good that fear should sit as the guardian of the soul, forcing it into wisdom; good that men should carry a threatening shadow in their hearts : else how should they learn to revere the right?" Expressed in a great variety of languages, that has been the fundamental doctrine of orthodoxy. It differs from our conception of ethical religion in that it denies to man the capacity to see and follow the right without the coercion of an external "guardian of the soul" or a "threatening shadow in their hearts." Freedom from religious fear is the first condition for ethical growth.

A second false value attributed to religion is its role as a preventive of radical political or economic movements. This role of religion in the social field is the counterpart of fear in the personal consciousness. In the year 1856 James J. Hill, a penniless youth of eighteen, came from Canada to the little town of St. Paul in Minnesota Territory. He became one of the greatest of the captains of industry in our post-Civil War days, building the Great Northern Railroad and contributing enormously to the growth of the Northwest from Lake Superior to the Pacific coast. Though an upright man, Mr. Hill never joined any religious body or interested himself in the creed or worship of any denomination. But he gave generously to religious institutions, establishing a Roman Catholic seminary in St. Paul and donating large sums to Protestant churches, in order, he said, "that the youth of the land might grow up under religious influences." In an address at the dedication of a building which he had given to a small college in Minnesota he said, "No nation can exist without a true religious spirit behind it. ... I hope to see the Decalogue in every schoolroom. The Bible will be the measure of the mental growth of this republic and of the prosperity of our nation." Thus we often hear a person say, "I don't belong to any religious body or go to any religious services myself, but I should not like to live in a town where there are no churches." This is a kind of absentee endorsement of religion as something good for the other fellow. It regards religion as a police force to preserve moral order. The police, of course, are necessary for the protection of the law-abiding members of society, but we do not look to them for ethical inspiration. Theirs is a negative function; whereas a true valuation of religion calls for the positive and continuous effort to contribute whatever strength and talent one has to the upbuilding of an ethical society. That is why those estimable people who refuse to identify themselves with an organization devoted to that purpose fail to set the highest value on religion. They remain on the sidelines while others are engaged in the contest, thus not only underestimating the contribution which their participation in the common effort might make, but also depriving themselves of the personal encouragement to ethical growth from the association with men and women striving for the knowledge and practice of the right.

There have been many other values attached to religion, some of them beneath contempt. St. Jerome in his fascinating letters tells of the dandified Roman priests of his day, with their perfumed locks, who besieged the doors of rich matrons to collect tribute. The hard-drinking, fox-hunting clergymen of eighteenth-century England prized their secure tenures in the Established Church and neglected the duty of furnishing spiritual nourishment to their congregations. "The hungry sheep looked up and were not fed." Deplorable, too, is the value set on religion by some snobbish people, as a mark of social distinction or even as an avenue to personal advantage. You remember the story of the poorly dressed man who was refused entrance by the usher of a fashionable church; and Jesus met him outside the door and said, "Never mind, my friend; I have been trying myself to get into that church for twenty years." A distant cousin of mine moved to New York some years ago to practice medicine, and was advised by a colleague that the best way to build up his practice was to join a wealthy church and if possible get the opportunity to pass the collection plate. But we have dwelt too long on these unworthy conceptions of the value of religion, which only go to show how liable this noblest sentiment of man is to abuse by the fear-monger, the self-righteous and the hypocrite. Let us rather ask what are the truly nourishing and enduring values in religion.

First of all, we must realize that religion appeals to men in a great variety of ways, according to the dominant tastes in the character of the individual. For the highly intellectual type of man, who seeks clarity of mind through logic and argument, the chief value of religion may lie in the efforts of the theologian to justify the ways of God to man. How many thousands of volumes, from the days of the early Christian apologists down, have been written to prove that the faith embodied in the creeds is compatible with the utmost reach of human reason! The more emotional type of person sets less value on religion as a body of belief supported by logic than on religion as a mystical experience in which he feels the presence of a divinity he cares not to attempt to define. We think of the great mathematician Einstein as a hard-headed scientist; but listen to what he writes in the volume of *Living Philosophies:* "The most beautiful thing we can experience is the mysterious. It is the source of all true art and science. He to whom the emotion is a stranger, who can no longer pause to wonder and stand rapt in awe, is as good as dead. His eyes are closed. ... To know that what is impenetrable to us really exists, manifesting itself as the highest wisdom and the most radiant beauty which our dull faculties can comprehend only in their most primitive forms—this feeling is at the center of true religiousness."

But there is danger in the overvaluation of the mystical element in religion, though I think all of us have felt at times Wordsworth's relief from "the weight of all this weary unintelligible world." And undue emphasis on mysticism is a form of escapism from the religious duty to give one's active support to the work of creating a better world. This duty cannot be done by immuring one's self in a monastery, like the author of *The Seven-storey Moun-*

tain, or retreating to the ivory tower of contemplation as a permanent residence. There is work for every citizen of good will to do, and that work is in the everyday world of the battle between hope and fear, light and darkness, right and wrong. There has yet to be eradicated from the teaching of the past the pernicious doctrine that the value of religion consists in the deliverance of man from contact with a doomed world. A better definition of religion is given by the writer of the Epistle of James: namely, to visit the fatherless and widows in their affliction and, while in the world, to keep one's self unspotted by its evil.

We of the ethical fellowship have a different conception of the enduring values of religion than any of the foregoing. We are not disturbed by the fear of punishment in a future existence, believing that wickedness brings its own punishment here in the shape of the deterioration of one's moral character. We have no urge to withdraw from society in order to escape from its burdens and distractions. We eschew the fruitless arguments of the theologians. Our meetings (to the distress of some members and the satisfaction of others) are as devoid of ceremony as the meetings of the Friends or the services of the Auld Scotch Kirk. What, then, are the enduring values which we find in religion? I would sum them up in the three following categories.

First of all, religion means, to me at least, the recognition of a supreme aim in life, to which every thought and deed is conformable, and the approximate attainment to which is the greatest satisfaction one can feel. This is not

ETHICS AS A RELIGION

a new doctrine discovered seventy-odd years ago by the founder of the ethical movement. He stood, as we do, in a long line of tradition, reaching back far beyond the Christian era to the Hebrew prophets who declared that what the Lord demanded of men was not ritual but righteousness, and centuries before the Hebrew prophets to the moral precepts of the Egyptian sages. Hear too these words of the Greek philosopher Aristotle, "the master of those who know," in his treatise on ethics: "If, therefore, among the ends at which our action aims there be one which we will for its own sake, while we will the others only for the sake of this, it is clear that this one ultimate end must be the Good, and indeed the supreme Good. Will not then a knowledge of the supreme Good be also of great importance for the conduct of life? Will it not better enable us to attain our proper object, like archers who have a target to aim at?" This is sound ethical doctrine. We too, like the ancient prophets of Israel and Greece and our modern forerunners like Roger Williams and Kant and Emerson, aim at the target of the supreme Good—"the ever increasing knowledge, love and practice of the right." Let us be heartened in our quest for this Good by the consciousness that we share, however unworthily, in the fellowship of those great souls who have insisted, often in the face of obloquy and persecution, that the only enduring value in religion is the contribution it makes to ethical growth.

Moreover, not only do we stand for the doctrine that

the pursuit of ethical enlightenment is the supreme end and aim of life, but we also have faith in man's capacity to pursue this aim independently of any theological creed or ceremonial ritual. It was an unfortunate moment in the history of religion when the theologians of the early Christian centuries elaborated the doctrine (so alien to the teaching of Jesus) of the utter incompetence of man to shape his destiny without accepting a scheme of salvation which virtually made him a pawn on the cosmic chess-board in a game between God and Satan. This ancient doctrine of human helplessness and defeatism, still preached by the evangelists, has diminished men's confidence in their ability to take in hand the courageous direction of their own destiny, and, by setting over them a master of their fate, has virtually denied their responsibility and substituted for religious freedom the profitless exercise of religious conformity.

Reverence is the keynote of religion. But reverence is not to be narrowed only to awe in the face of impenetrable mystery, much less to acquiescence in the dogmas which satisfied the religious cravings of men of bygone ages. "Merit lives from man to man," and the widespread assertion that moral excellence is a mere corollary of belief in creed or ceremony has been disproved throughout history by the host of noble and upright men and women who have made no profession of the faith of church or temple. Not that the value of religion consists in negation. There is a faith which transcends the divisive creeds of Christendom, which have hitherto inspired enough religion to make men and nations hate one another, but not enough to make them love one another.

We plead for the dawn of this transcendent faith. We find the enduring value of religion in reverence for the unrealized but latent worth in every human being. We believe that the elicitation of that worth in others by conduct which at the same time enhances the worth that is in ourselves is the supreme test of our religion. We fix our spiritual sights not on the gulden streets and pearly gates of a remote heaven, but on the building of the city of light on this earth. We look forward to the time, perhaps centuries away, perhaps through the folly of man never to come, when faith in the overarching importance of the mutual stimulation of people's best possibilities is as common to mankind as is now faith in the traditional doctrines of the traditional religions. And when that time shall have come, civilization will have advanced as far beyond its present state as we have advanced since the days of man's first appearance on earth.

CHAPTER SIXTEEN

THE FUTURE
OF ETHICAL RELIGION

W E STUDY the past not only because of our perennial interest in a human story, but also because the past is the only guide we have for a forecast of the future. Not that the past furnishes us with specific answers to the problems before us, for every age has its peculiar problems which arise out of a complexity of causes. However, in every field of human interest it is the future which is the primary concern of endeavor. The statesman works to secure a future for his country in harmony with the ideals which he has received from the founders of the republic. The educator seeks to arouse in his students a sense of their future responsibilities as free and privileged citizens. The physician, the biochemist, the psychiatrist all labor to improve the health and sanity of future generations. Even the scourges of the human race entertain grandiose plans for the future. Hitler predicted a thousand years of Nazi domination; Mussolini dreamed of restoring the glory and despotism of the Roman Empire. Thus, though "the shape of things to come" can never be clear and sharp in its outline, it is the vision which beckons us all—the American dream, the better world, the age of brotherhood, the dawn of peace. Without such vision peoples perish and the individual loses the chief stimulus to a life of service. To live "in the present" has no meaning except to live for the future.

The definitions of religion have been many and varied. The history of religion has been an epic of mingled splendor and squalor, of compassion and cruelty, of sincerity and superstition, of noble self-sacrifice and base hypocrisy. But whatever varieties of form or vagaries of behavior religion has shown, one constant feature may be confidently posited of them all: namely, that they owe their origin to man's desire for his soul's peace. It is impossible to think that men should either invent or adopt a religion for the purpose of confusing, oppressing or in-

THE FUTURE OF ETHICAL RELIGION

juring themselves. That would be a contradiction in terms. And this fact of the origin of religion in some sort of aspiration is as true of what we call the lower and cruder manifestations of superstition and magic as it is of the nobler types, like original Buddhism with its desire to be freed from mundane illusions, or Judaism with its thirst to be delivered from sin through obedience to the perfect law of Jehovah, or Christianity with its quest for the peace that passeth understanding in the consciousness of sonship with God. The savage who leaps into the air in his religious dance to encourage the corn to sprout, or chews tough bark to soften the heart of a woman, or hangs a curtain before his hut to keep evil spirits from entering, is in his own peculiar way invoking "metaphysical aid" in his search for deliverance from impotence and fear. Yet today we mark this strange paradox—that for thousands of people religion is a cause of great mental confusion, of widespread doubt, and of soul-sickness, rather than an agency of comfort and assurance. What is the cause of this sinister transformation? Why has religion become for many an incubus instead of an inspiration? These are questions of the utmost moment. They go to the very depths of our nature. To answer them is not easy; but to refuse to attempt to answer them is to dodge the most important challenge to the human mind.

I believe that the chief cause of the confessedly confused and apologetic status of religion today is the failure to discriminate between the competing *kinds* of religion that are offered for our acceptance. In May of 1919 some sixty-five hundred orthodox ministers and laymen gathered at Philadelphia and formed the World's Christian Fundamentals Association, publishing a volume under the title *God Hath Spoken.* It summed up God's oracles in a number of "points," the most important of which were the verbal inspiration and inerrancy of the Old and New Testaments, the doctrine of the Trinity, the virgin birth, the utter corruption of man, the bodily resurrection of Jesus, his imminent return to earth, and the eternal bliss of the saved in heaven and the eternal conscious suffering of the lost in hell. In an article in *Current History* of June, 1927, by W. B. Riley, a Baptist minister, the author lashes out in a vicious attack on modernism, Darwinism and deism, and calls for a "fight to the finish, asking no quarter from the world, the flesh and the devil." "No cowards are wanted here," he cries; "no clever compromisers with the treacherous spirit of the age; no cunning contrivers who practice the art of upholding the truth in uprightness; no renegades who hold back their gospel weapons from attack, while doing the popular works which win the applause of men. Keep out, all of you! The object of this Confederacy is to raise up and gather a host whose faith shall be a challenge to the world's unbelief." As unashamed "upholders of uprightness," we are perfectly willing to "keep out" of the Reverend Mr. Riley's company of fundamentalists.

In contrast to the dour dogmatism of fundamentalism the Roman Catholic Church offers a more amiable kind of religion. Its slogan is not "keep out" but come in. When

THE FUTURE OF ETHICAL RELIGION

Professor Charles A. Briggs of Union Theological Seminary was charged with heresy about a half a century ago by the Presbyterian Church, on account of his higher criticism of the Old Testament, he received letters from prominent Catholic prelates inviting him to join their communion and assuring him that he would not be disturbed for any views he might hold on the book of Genesis. Yet, for all the urbanity of the Catholic priesthood, the church is adamant in its insistence on Catholicism as the only true faith, into whose fold the rebellious Protestant sects (cut-offs) will eventually be brought. For the Catholic the church, not the Bible, is the paramount authority (as St. Augustine proclaimed many centuries ago), and the chief offense is not heresy but schism—the rending of the sacred garment of Christ. A strange paradox arises from this centralization of authority in the hierarchy culminating in the pope. For on the one hand the church is a democracy in its welcome to men of all classes and its provision of a career open to talents; while, on the other hand, once a man is admitted to the priesthood, he finds himself in a totalitarian system as uncompromising as the Communism against which it fights. No better illustration of this duality could be found than in the papal pronouncement reported from Rome by Mr. Cianfarra in the New York *Times* of February 28, 1950. Pope Pius XII "allowed" the Catholic clergy to discuss with representatives of non-Catholic Christian bodies means of pooling their spiritual strength to combat Communism. But he made it clear that the traditional position of the Catholic Church, which considers itself the mother church and all non-Catholic denominations schismatic, was "unchanged," and that the possibility of collaboration among Christians was "limited exclusively to questions other than faith and morals." How such a limitation could be reconciled with his previous invitation to Catholics and non-Catholics to "pool their spiritual strength" is hard to see. And what kind of discussion that omitted "questions of faith and morals" could have the slightest effect in combating Communism? Catholics, Protestants and Jews may meet in a spirit of gentlemanly kindness and good will to find some common ground of unity; but, however heartily they may co-operate in charitable works and social reform, they never can find a common religious ground so long as one party repudiates and another party recognizes a totalitarian pope who sets an arbitrary limit to discussion and exercises an authority as absolute as that of Stalin. Nay, more absolute, since it is exercised by one who claims to be the vice-regent of God on earth.

The more liberal and modernistic types of religion shun both the dogmatic truculence of the fundamentalists and the stark authoritarianism of the Catholics. Their ministers stress moral rather than confessional requirements. Yet they halt midway on the road to emancipation from religious formalities which have lost meaning for the age in which we live. They no longer stoke the fires of hell or use hymns which call men worthless worms. But they do not come out unequivocally against the old creeds on which their churches were built. Their sincerity is not to be questioned; but do they realize that there is no logical halfway house between orthodoxy and complete religious freedom? The Reformed Jews, as we have seen from the quotation from Professor Klausner in an earlier chapter, also hold to the doctrine of a peculiar sanctity for the Law of Moses, while acknowledging that in many of its provisions it has lost significance for our age. The followers of all these types of religion, fundamentalists, Catholics, modernists, and Jews, quite naturally believe that the future of religion belongs to them—to say nothing of the Christian Scientists, the Bahaists, the Quakers, and the rest who make up the nearly two hundred religious sects of our country. What reason have we of the Ethical fellowship to believe, in the midst of all this welter of faiths, that ours can lay a claim to be the religion of the future?

Before attempting to answer this question let me warn the reader of two trends which must be resolutely fought against if religion is to have more vitality in the future than it appears to have at the present time. The first is what Gilbert Highet in his remarkable book on *The Classical Heritage* calls "our naive confidence in applied science which deters us from thinking out problems as earnestly as our forefathers did in conversation, debate and meditation." "Things are in the saddle and ride mankind," wrote Emerson. "Glory to man in the highest, for man is the master of things," wrote Swinburne. But it is not man's *things* that constitute his glory. Perhaps the most persistent illusion that social well-being or personal happiness can be attained by any devices that ignore the ethical element is the belief, so widely held in this materialistic age, that a rise in the economic standard of living will automatically usher in a social millennium. Certainly, no one would deny that an income sufficient to provide a family with decent home and food and clothing adequate for the protection of health is an indispensable factor in building a wholesome society. But an indispensable factor must not be confused with a total product. Man is much more than a body needing food, raiment, rest and recreation. A rise in the material standard of living can bring him these things but is no guarantee in itself of an increase in his moral stature. Would a raise of ten dollars a week in wages change an untruthful man into a truthful one, or an envious man into a generous one? Do those most amply supplied with the material goods of life offer us the best examples of the virtues of unselfishness, uprightness and the love of their fellow men? Is material prosperity the best school of humility? Moreover, the much heralded standard of living is no standard at all, but a most variable conception, according to the economic status of the people who debate it. The constant struggle between capital and labor is proof of this. For every demand for an increase in wages is urged on the ground that it is necessary to protect the workers' standard of living and resisted on the ground that it would be ruinous to the employers' standard of living.

Furthermore, science, for all the benefits that its discoveries bestow on man in lightening his labors and alleviating his diseases, can never furnish the vital spark that kindles his moral endeavor. The scientist, qua scientist, is ethically neutral. It is a matter of indifference to him whether the steel which he turns out goes to build girders for a hospital for the saving of life or guns for a battleship for the destruction of life. The Curies toiled amid disheartening difficulties before they succeeded in the discovery of radium; but they never dreamed that their discovery would pave the way for the manufacture of the deadliest weapon ever placed in human hands. Nor can one imagine that the modest Robert Oppenheimer, conducting the tryout of the first atomic bomb on the New Mexican desert, anticipated that the instrument would be used to wipe out the lives of tens of thousands of Japanese civilians in Hiroshima and Nagasaki. Science provides the means, but ethics determines the ends for which the means are used. And the unworthy ends to which potentially noble means are so often put are a constant threat to our intellectual and moral standards. We are solicited only to listen and look, not to read and think. For hours on hours the radio and television conspire to cultivate

> *The ear to no grave harmonies inclined,*
> *The eye to all majestic meaning blind.*

In addition to the undiscriminating worship of applied science, a second disturbing trend in our day is the diminishing confidence in the merits and destiny of what Washington called "the republican model of government." The assaults on democracy in the last generation have been bitter and unrelenting. Wars, persecutions, proscriptions, deportations have robbed whole peoples' sense of security in which alone a democratic society can flourish, and dictators have capitalized on the resultant moral paralysis to lure millions into sacrificing their dignity as free men for the delusive promise of happiness under a regime of suspicion, coercion, proscription and total regimentation. The poison of antidemocratic ideologies has spread to our country. Never before in our history has there been such a ferment of fear and anxiety as we find today. The papers run column after column of news of trials of spies, fellow-travelers, filchers of state documents, perjurers, delators. Committees of Congress spend hours hearing the testimony of accusation and defense. The Department of State is charged with harboring traitors in its employ. The regents of the University of California compel the four thousand members of the faculty to subscribe to an oath repudiating Communism. It seems as though the spirit of the Holy Inquisition had seized upon the land.

Now these remarks on science and democracy have a direct relevance to the future of ethical religion. For, in the first place, while not inimical to science, religion finds no support in science except the negative support of the elimination of the ignorance and superstitions which have so often sullied the religions of the past. The *Sian vital* which gives religion its strength and nurture is an act of faith, transcending but not rejecting the findings of science. And secondly, ethical religion and democracy are complementary institutions, the basic idea in each being the dignity of man—an idea which includes both his liberty and his corresponding responsibility. Wherever the former is restricted or the latter neglected both religion and democracy are impaired. Unfortunately, the traditional religions contain elements which have been unfavorable, to say the least, to both these requisites of democracy. On the one hand, almost every battle for the freedom of thought has had to be fought against an authority claiming divine sanction; and on the other hand, man's responsibility has been weakened by the doctrine of his impotence to pursue a course of righteousness of his own volition. The wonderful adventure of winning through to independence by self-discipline, the adventure of democracy, has been denied him. But he cannot tolerate in this day a hobble to his religious freedom any more than he can tolerate a threat to his political freedom. The modem age has brought a situation in which not only the hope but the necessity of building a new society confronts us. Passive endurance may have been a virtue in the times when men had no chance of improving their lot of slavery or serfdom. What is called for now is a determined, venturesome, aggressive spirit to go forward and redeem us from the frailties and follies which have brought the world to the brink of disaster. We must have a religion which squares with this spirit of adventure. As Professor Max Otto has daringly but truthfully said, "We must engage in the task of making God safe for democracy." Blasphemy! cry the fundamentalists. But the fundamentalist Athenians put Socrates to death as a blasphemer when he tried to substitute a god of reason for the mythological gods which the city worshiped; and the fundamentalist scribes and Pharisees had Jesus crucified as a blasphemer because he transcended the narrow prescriptions of the Law of Moses. Blasphemy has ever been the charge of autocracy against democracy, whether of political, economic or religious autocrats. The road to progress has been lined with the offensive billboards of reaction, prejudice and denunciation. Let us glance at them and press resolutely forward. We know that democracy has the defects of its qualities. As it is the highest form of society that civilization has attained, so it is the hardest to maintain in its ideal effectiveness. But for all its shortcomings, we are pledged to its survival; and we can echo the witty aphorism of Winston Churchill, "Democracy is the worst of governments—except those that have been proposed to succeed it."

In the year 1831 Alexis de Tocqueville, a young French nobleman, was sent to America by the government of Louis Philippe ostensibly to study the prisons of our country. But his interests went far beyond penal institutions, and the book which he published, *On Democracy in America,* was the most penetrating analysis of our government and society to appear before James Bryce's *American Commonwealth* a half a century later. "There are sometimes periods in the life of a nation," wrote de Tocqueville, "when public morality is destroyed, religious belief shaken, and the spell of tradition broken." Such a period he believed he saw in the revolutionary ferment of the Jacksonian era into which he was introduced. And such a period we are living in today. The moral imperatives which were stressed by our forefathers have become affected with relativism and optionalism. Religion has become largely a matter of convention and conservatism. The "twin pillars" of morality and religion which George Washington saw upholding the temple of American democracy are attacked by the termites of materialistic indifference. But since freedom can live only in the atmosphere of democracy, and ethical religion can thrive only where complete freedom of thought and speech prevails, it is obvious that the interdependence of democracy and ethical religion is a necessary condition for the preservation and perpetuation of our religious heritage. Do the traditional forms of religion, Catholic, Protestant or Jewish, satisfy this condition? One has only to read Paul Blanshard's carefully documented *American Freedom and Catholic Power* to be convinced of the complete domination of the priesthood not only over the articles of faith of the church but over a great number of fields in which secular control has gradually extended its sway, such as education, medicine, law, labor and sex. The Protestant sects and Jewish congregations, though lacking the totalitarian claims of the Roman Church, still cling (in their official creeds, at least) to doctrines which are logically incompatible with the actual beliefs of the most enlightened of their ministers and rabbis.

I know that even to suggest the possibility of a religion beyond Judaism and Christianity will be thought by de-

ETHICS AS A RELIGION

vout Jews and Christians nothing less than blasphemy, so ingrained has the custom become of identifying religion with their own form of it. But the student of the history of religion recognizes that many a religion older than Judaism or Christianity has given place to a new type more in accord with the developing march of science and humanitarianism. Man's task is endless to build an ever better society on earth, and the most important part of that task is the search for a religion which shall not only accord with his increasing knowledge of the world in which he lives, but shall also enlist his deepest devotion to spiritual growth. We believe that the time has come when religion needs a new embodiment. "It is certain," says Dr. A. Eustace Haydon, "that none of the traditional religions is adequate. Their thought forms and techniques of salvation belong to a world that is no more. Even their practical codes which remained stable through many changes in theology are now shattered by the economic and political forces playing upon them, and can no longer give guidance as a way of life or security for the individual. It may be necessary for the old forms of religion to die that religion may live." These are bold words from the leader of the Chicago Ethical Society, and they will be disputed by those who believe that the current forms of religion are fixed and final. But there are many people in the churches who are in intellectual and emotional sympathy with the kind of religion which would shift the emphasis from theology to ethics. Even some priests of the Catholic Church have incurred the rebuke of their superiors by

THE FUTURE OF ETHICAL RELIGION

leaning to the side of liberality. And outside that church the hurling of denunciations and anathemas against supporters of dissenting sects, which was so common a generation or two ago, has mostly ceased. The denominations now live together in a friendly rivalry of mutual proselytism.

In our conviction that ethical religion will eventually displace the types of religion which put the prime importance on the confession of creed or the performance of ritual, we are not animated by any spirit of hostility to the churches. We readily acknowledge both the great services which Judaism and Christianity have rendered mankind and the sincerity and devotion of the vast majority of their rabbis, priests and ministers. We would agree that Judaism and Christianity are higher forms of religion than the old paganism which they conquered or their contemporary rivals in the world. But such recognition does not absolve us from the duty of pleading for what we believe to be a still higher type of religion. The better is enemy of the best, and, as Tennyson wrote, "One needs must love the highest when one sees it." Nor do we labor under the illusion that the new religion which we advocate will make a speedy conquest. Ecclesiastical institutions with great wealth and tremendous power have a tenacious hold on millions of people, and even though their vitality be weakened by the progress of science and rationalism, they may be expected to retain for long a large part of their authority.

But the unmistakable trend of religion is toward a diminishing stress on creed and ceremony and a corresponding emphasis on ethics. The almost exclusive concern for one's personal salvation which was the theme of the old Puritan divines and is the theme of the revivalists today is yielding to a conception of religion as a social agency to inspire in men a zeal for the mutual elicitation of their best natures and a finer discrimination between the true and the false values of life. Our confidence in the future prevalence of a purely ethical religion, be it near or distant, is based on the following three propositions:

First, it is the only type of religion that comports wholly with a democratic form of society; and as we stake our faith on the permanence of such a society, so must we be devoted to a kind of religion which fits it.

Second, ethical religion accepts without cavil or reservations the facts of science as they are progressively discovered and tested, confident that, however disturbing they may be to traditional dogmas, they can never deprive men of the spiritual aspirations which have been and will continue to be the source and origin of all the higher religions.

And third, and most important, ethical religion is the only religion that can unite men of every race and clime. Creeds are divisive; ethics is universal. What men of good will are seeking today with an earnestness never so anxious before is a way to bring the unity of nations out of the divisiveness which threatens to wreck our dearly bought civilization. United Nations, Union Now, World Union, World Government, World Federation are the slogans in the fight for a world free from hatred, destitution and war. Could anything contribute more to victory in this fight than the advent of a religion which eliminated the divisive elements of creed and ritual and summoned us to hear and obey the noble words which St. Paul spoke on the hill at Athens: "He hath made of one blood all nations of men for to dwell on the earth."

EPILOGUE

THE FOUNDING OF THE ETHICAL MOVEMENT

The following account of the origin and aims of the Ethical Culture movement is offered for those who wish to have information on the subject.

FELIX ADLER was born in the summer of 1851 in the little town of Alzey in the Rhineland. Six years later his father, Rabbi Samuel Adler, brought his family to America in response to an invitation to serve Temple Emanu-El in New York. Felix was graduated from Columbia College at the age of nineteen, and was sent to

Germany to study for the rabbinate, with a view to his becoming the associate or the successor of his father. But his three years at the universities of Berlin and Heidelberg (where he took his doctor's degree) undermined his faith in the Hebrew religion. He returned to New York in 1873 to preach one sermon in his father's temple, which was his valedictory sermon. He then accepted the appointment to a professorship of Semitic languages and literature at Cornell University. In spite of his lifelong interest in education, as shown by his founding of the Ethical Culture Schools and his tenure of a professorship of ethics at Columbia for the last thirty years of his life (1903-1933), the urge to preach was so strong in him that he resigned his post at Cornell, and in the spring of 1876 was back in New York. A small group of men from the synagogue, who shared his religious views, had joined with him on his return from Germany in a Union for the Higher Life, which stressed the three points of sexual purity, the elevation of the working class, and intellectual development. Under his leadership they formed the New York Society for Ethical Culture in May, 1876, and for more than fifty years Felix Adler expounded his ethical religion in Sunday morning addresses to ever increasing audiences. Early in the present century the Society moved from Carnegie Hall to its own commodious meetinghouse at West Sixty-fourth Street and Central Park West, designed by Robert D. Kohn, sometime president of the American Association of Architects and for many years president of the Society.

ETHICS AS A RELIGION

In the mid-1880's Ethical Societies were established in Philadelphia, Chicago and St. Louis; and in more recent years in Brooklyn, New Rochelle, Washington, Newark and Los Angeles. These Societies are now federated in the American Ethical Union, and have a combined membership of some four thousand. The movement spread to foreign lands: England, France, Germany, Austria and Japan; but except in England the war put an end to its growth. A flourishing Society in Vienna was dissolved by Hitler and its leaders were thrown into a concentration camp. They were rescued through the personal intervention of Dr. John L. Elliott, Dr. Adler's senior assistant, and brought to America. After eleven years Dr. Boemer returned to Vienna (1949) and resuscitated the Society there. Groups of people in several cities are eager to form Ethical Societies, but it is difficult to find trained leaders to send to them. A cherished project of Dr. Adler's was the establishment of an institution for the training of ethical leaders; but neither the funds nor the personnel have been forthcoming for such a project.

The Sunday morning services, important as they are, are by no means the only activities of the Ethical Societies. In 1880 a "Workingman's School" was started in New York with free tuition. A decade later tuition was charged; but, in order to preserve the democratic character of the school, the policy of full or partial scholarships for at least a third of the students was adopted. Instruction in ethics was given in all the grades. A former president of the Board of Education of the city said, "If I could have my way, every public school in this city would be conducted in accordance with the system adopted in this school." The Brooklyn Society also has a flourishing school, built up by the devoted services through many years of the leader of the Society, Dr. Henry Neumann, and his wife. Though the other Societies do not have Ethical Culture Schools, they carry on educational work in their neighborhood houses and in their clubs. In 1928 the magnificent Fieldston School (also designed by Mr. Kohn) was opened, overlooking the Hudson. It has an unrivaled reputation as a preparatory school, and a list of graduates who have done honor to the various colleges and universities to which they have gone.

The social contributions of the Societies to the life of their communities have been various and valuable. Settlement houses, like Hudson Guild and Madison House in New York, Henry Booth House in Chicago, and Southwark House in Philadelphia, have exerted a wholesome influence on the underprivileged youth of the city tenements and streets. The civic activities of the leaders of the Societies have been too numerous to list. Dr. Adler, to mention a few of his services, was a member of the tenement house commission and the Lexow Committee for the suppression of vice, an arbiter sought and respected in labor disputes, and for many years president of the Child Study Association. Mr. W. Edwin Collier is a charter member of the United Nations Council of Philadelphia and secretary of the Marriage Council of that city. Mr. William M. Salter, for many years leader of the Chicago

Ethical Society, braved obloquy by his plea for a fair trial for the anarchists charged with the responsibility for the Haymarket Riot of 1886; and Dr. Horace Bridges, leader emeritus of the same Society, was for years the protagonist for the rights of Negroes in the Urban League. The venerable Mr. Percival Chubb, leader emeritus of the St. Louis Society, identified himself with every movement for civic betterment, and his successor, Mr. J. Hutton Hynd, supplemented his preaching and pastoral duties with teaching at the university and giving radio broadcasts. Other activities of the Societies have been summer camps, district nursing, festivals, play schools, reading circles, and numerous clubs. A recent institution, inaugurated by Algernon D. Black, executive leader of the New York Society, and sponsored by the American Ethical Union, is the Encampment for Citizenship, which brings together about one hundred twenty-five people from all parts of the country each summer at Fieldston for study and recreation.

The Ethical Societies have no creed. Their only requirement for membership is the devotion to ethics as the supreme end of life. The individual is free to entertain whatever philosophical or theological beliefs appeal to him. Nor are the leaders bound to hold the views of their colleagues on political, social or economic questions. Naturally, the religious philosophy set forth in the writings of Dr. Adler, especially in his chief work, *An Ethical Philosophy of Life,* is an invaluable guide for the leaders and for those members of the Societies who study it; but it

THE FOUNDING OF THE ETHICAL MOVEMENT

is in no sense a "Bible" of the movement, like Mrs. Eddy's *Science and Health.* In his Preface Dr. Adler modestly wrote: "This book records a philosophy of life growing out of the experience of a lifetime. The convictions put in it are not dogmatic, for dogma is the conviction of one man imposed authoritatively upon others. The convictions herein expounded are submitted to those who search, as the writer has searched, for light on the problems of life, in order that they may compare their experience with his, and their interpretations of their experience with his interpretations." Nevertheless, we shall get a clearer idea of the principles which underlie the movement from Dr. Adler's writings than from any other source. We may sum up those principles in the following points.

1. Basic to an ethical concept of religion is belief in a universal and indefeasible moral law. Human reason cannot "prove" the existence of such a law; but the greatest thinkers of all time have recognized it as normative for men's conduct. Plato saw it as the eternal heavenly pattern of the good, the beautiful and the true of which we on earth have only a dim perception, owing to the handicap of our material bodies. It inspired in Kant an awe as profound as did the contemplation of "the starry heavens." The moral law is not written in the statutes of parliaments nor handed down in a single divine revelation. It is revealed progressively in the effort to obey it. Therefore man's supreme duty, as well as his supreme satisfaction, lies in fulfilling the moral law to the best of his powers. Some call this getting "in tune with the infi-

nite," others living according to nature, others still doing the will of God. But whether the approach be philosophical, naturalistic or mystical, the end remains the same: namely, the recognition of and obedience to the universal moral law.

2. The way in which we testify to our reverence for the moral law is through our relations with our fellows in the family, the social circle, business and professions. The orthodox have always insisted that a man's first duty was to "get right with God." We do not decry the need of repentance for our misdoings. It should be a constant spur to better living. But when the Psalmist cries, "Against thee, thee only have I sinned and done this evil in thy sight," we cannot agree with him. The sins we do are sins against our fellow men, and the repentance has value only in its effect on our relations with them. For "merit lives from man to man." Did not Jesus himself make the resolve to lead a more righteous life the test of the genuineness of repentance? Not those who cried "Lord, Lord!" entered the kingdom of heaven, but those who *did* the will of God. It was not enough for him to say, "Thy sins be forgiven thee"; he added, "Go, and sin no more." I am not here questioning the help that people feel they get from prayer or ritual in their effort to lead a more worthy life. My only plea is that any kind of religious ceremony that does not eventuate in ethical conduct deserves no better name than superstition.

3. Another basic proposition of ethical religion is the attribution of worth to every human being. This is an act

of faith, like the belief in a universal moral law. Of course, we do not mean that every man and woman is valuable to society. There are drunkards, thieves and murderers. What we do mean is that even in the most depraved of men there is a latent worth which may be brought out by some regenerative experience, as has been shown in many an instance. Our belief in the intrinsic worth of the individual stems from the conception of human society as a body of induplicable members (Dr. Adler called it the *corpus spirituale*), each of whom is necessary to the completion of the whole. Moreover, it is by the attribution of worth to others that we become cognizant of the potential worth in ourselves. Deep calls unto deep. No two human beings are exactly alike either in physical traits or in moral endowment. And it is this uniqueness of personality that makes each individual an induplicable member of society. We sometimes say that when Nature makes a great man, like Lincoln, she breaks the mold; but she does that for every man, the most obscure and "forgotten," who comes into the world. Thus we become conscious of our own uniqueness, with the moral obligations it imposes, only through the recognition that we are members of a community of unique individuals. Note particularly that by "worth" we do not mean a man's intellectual achievements or his social amenities; much less the accumulated fortune which is referred to when men say, Mr. X was worth fifty million. We do not, like the cloistered monk, spurn the social contacts out of which the amenities of life develop, but regard them only as the surface manifestation of a personality whose real significance lies in the recognition and cultivation of the spiritual nature which is man's birthright.

4. Of course, the concept of the inestimable worth of the individual is not a doctrine peculiar to ethical religion. The ancient Stoics believed that every man contained a spark of the divine. The parable of the lost sheep illustrates the emptiness of the fold so long as a single one is outside its shelter. The distinctive factor in our ethical doctrine is the emphasis which it puts on the reciprocal influence of character upon character. The founder of the movement expressed this idea in a formula which has become a guide for the members: namely, "So act as to elicit the best in others, and by so doing elicit the best in thyself." This ethical imperative differs from the famous categorical imperative of Kant, which bids us so act that our conduct might be taken as a universal norm. For no man's conduct can be free from faults, however eagerly he may strive to eliminate them. The Kantian formula smacks therefore of egotism. Nor does the Golden Rule quite satisfy the ethical requirement. To do unto others as we would have them do unto us sounds too much like a bargain, besides setting up our own desires as the standard for our neighbor's deeds. On the other hand, the ethical formula stresses the need of both self and neighbor for the help to better living which the elicitation of the best in each can furnish. We acknowledge the inestimable worth of another by appealing in word and action to the latent

excellence in him, and at the same time release in ourselves latent powers of moral growth.

These four principles of the recognition of a universal moral law, the fulfillment of that law in human relationships, the infinite worth of the induplicable individual, and the mutual elicitation of the best in others and so in ourselves as the rule of conduct, are basic to our conception of ethical religion. Needless to say that their application in political policy, labor relations and social intercourse would transform the distressful world in which we live into one worthy of the vision of those

> *immortal servants of mankind,*
> *Who from their graves watch by how slow degrees*
> *The world-soul broadens with the centuries.*

There are certain misconceptions of the nature and aims of the ethical movement which should be corrected. First, it is charged with a hostile attitude toward religion, and is itself denied the name of a religion. It is true that there are many doctrines and practices of the churches that we do not approve; but it is because we th<u>ink</u> them inharmonious with the present scientific and humanitarian age, rather than because we have any positive enmity against them. We believe that religion is no more exempt from criticism and amendment than is any other interest of humanity. It would be entirely misleading, for example, to regard the men who advocated the Copemican system of astronomy as animated by hatred against the earlier theory of Ptolemy, or the founders of modern medicine as "hostile" to Galen or Hippocrates. The older conceptions were simply outgrown. They no longer fitted the physical facts revealed by science. So the once generally accepted religious doctrines of the churches have been rendered ineffective by new developments in social theory and new insights into the psychic nature of man. It is for a religion to fit the age that we seek. And an unbiased reading of the writings and addresses of the leaders of the Ethical Societies will show that they are not animated by a spirit of hostility to Judaism or Christianity. On the contrary, they are ready to acknowledge the consolation and inspiration which these religions have furnished for millions of people, and to preserve and appropriate their ethical content. But no church can have a monopoly on religion. They are all products of the search of their founders and continuators, in the historical environment of their time, for an answer to the universal and persistent question of man's duty and destiny.

The orthodox churches claim to have the answer, confirmed by divine revelation. They are not seekers for the truth, but possessors of the truth. Hence they interpret inability to accept the authority of their hierarchy or their creeds as an attack of the dissidents on religion itself. For example, Catholic priests in their sermons and radio broadcasts constantly excoriate liberals as "godless," "rebels," "presumptuous," "self-righteous" and "emissaries of Satan." The Ethical Societies have come in for a good share of such denunciation. The fundamentalists have been little less severe in their diatribes, and other Protestant groups, while more moderate in their language, have been no more willing to accord us the status of a religious body. If the test of religion is the acceptance of a creed or obedience to a priestly authority, then our critics are right. But no display of pomp and ceremony, no ecclesiastical power or prestige, no weight of numbers can shake our belief that true religion consists in the fulfillment, to the extent of our powers, of our duties to our fellow men, whatever philosophical or theological views we may hold. We do not attack conventional religion: we simply find that it has no inspiration for us. "Which of the religions do I follow?" asks Schiller in one of his aphorisms. "None, and why? Because of my religion."

Another charge sometimes brought against the Ethical Societies is that their members consider themselves a select group somewhat superior to their neighbors. This misconception is perhaps chiefly due to a false interpretation of the phrase "ethical culture" in the title of the movement. And to correct it, some of the Societies have omitted the word "culture." What was meant by the word was not that we think of ourselves as a cultured group in the ordinary sense of the term, but that our aim is the cultivation of ethics. A culture in the biological meaning of the word is a medium adapted for the growth of a plant or any other form of life that it is desirable to nurture. That is the sense in which we use the word. Nor do we mean by the word "ethical" that we have attained a moral stature superior to that of other men. The very devotion with which we seek growth in ethical thought and action is proof of the great gap we recognize between our accomplishment and our aspiration. Is the seeker for truth less modest or humble than the man who professes to have the truth? Was Roger Williams a less worthy exemplar of religion than the cocksure Puritan divines of Massachusetts who drove him out of the colony? It seems to me that if the opprobrious charge of a feeling of superiority to one's neighbor is to be brought against anyone, it fits best the man who thinks of himself as "saved" and his neighbor as "lost." The old church father Tertullian, as we have seen, said that one of the joys of heaven would be to look over the ramparts and behold the suffering of sinners in hell. Jonathan Edwards preached a sermon on the text: The tortures of their husbands in hell no cause of grief to their wives in heaven. These, of course, are extreme examples of ethical perversity. But they show how dangerous to true religion is the kind of self-congratulation that can too often be observed in people who believe that they have attained to righteousness.

The criticism is often made that the services of the Ethical Societies lack warmth. There is no participation of the audience in them; the addresses from the platform are too intellectual; the fundamental religious principles of the movement are not sufficiently emphasized. We might answer these criticisms in reverse order. First, although the leaders and guest speakers deal with a great variety of subjects (political, educational, economic, historical, etc.), these subjects are all treated from the point

THE FOUNDING OF THE ETHICAL MOVEMENT

of view of their ethical implications. An address on labor relations, for example, would not be so much concerned with the grievances of the workers or the mechanics of a conciliation board as with showing the effect upon both employer and employee of approaching the problem in the ethical spirit of mutual respect for the human worth of the personalities engaged. If a popular book was selected for the subject of the morning's discourse, it would be because the book presented an important ethical problem, and "author meets critic" would mean that the author met a critic of his moral stand and not of his literary style, or cleverness of construction. As to the alleged overemphasis on the speakers' intellectuality, so far as it is deserved I think it rather a compliment than a reproach. "Come, let us reason together" is our invitation to our audience, and we respect their desire for edification by putting our best thought into our addresses.

It is true that there is little vocal participation of the audience in our services. A few of the Societies have congregational singing or responsive readings. But we have no litany, no robed choirs, no recited creed, no genuflections. Some of our members think the service is too bare; others would eliminate such meager ceremonial as we have. The usual program for the morning meeting consists of a reading appropriate to the subject of the address, the address itself, and a closing word as a benediction, with music before and after the service and in the intervals of the program. More than a century ago Emerson prophesied that the new church which he foresaw would be "founded on moral science, at first cold and naked, a babe in a manger; . . . but it will have heaven and earth for its beams and rafters; science for symbol and illustration; it will fast enough gather beauty, music, picture, poetry." The prophecy still waits fulfillment.

Because the founder of the ethical movement was a Jew many people have jumped to the conclusion that it is a Jewish sect. The same argument might apply to Christianity, for Jesus was a Jew; St. Paul, who established the church, called himself "a Hebrew of the Hebrews"; and the early apostles were all Jews. A prominent humanist, when asked the difference between humanism and Ethical Culture, replied, "Humanism has a Christian background and Ethical Culture a Jewish background," without considering that Christianity itself had a Jewish background. But Felix Adler broke as completely with Jewish theology and ceremonial as did Jesus or St. Paul. It is not the accident of one's birth that determines one's religion—at least for people who think for themselves. Moreover, all the four "original" lieutenants of Dr. Adler were Gentiles who came out of the Christian church: S. Bums Weston, William M. Salter, Walter Sheldon, and Stanton Coit, who founded the Ethical Societies of Philadelphia, Chicago, St. Louis, and London respectively. Their successors in the leadership of these Societies (Collier, Bridges, Haydon, Hynd, Blackham) have all been non-Jews. To call Ethical Culturists members of a Jewish sect is as gross a misconception as it would be to call them members of a Masonic order. Ethical religion acknowledges with gratitude the contributions which the Hebrew prophets and the Christian clergy have made to the moral and spiritual uplift of humanity. These are treasures which are not to be monopolized by any church or sect. They belong to us all. But with them are mixed many untimely survivals of creed and ritual which are like the detritus that is borne down with the life-giving waters of a stream. Constant purification of the waters is necessary to preserve religion as a vital, pervasive and inspiring influence in man's life.

> *Mid changing systems, fading creeds,*
> *That fail us in our deepest needs,*
> *Our striving souls refuse to rest*
> *And call our present good the best.*
> *Our eyes in rapture seem to see*
> *A mightier faith that is to be.*
>
> *Our fathers' faith we do not slight;*
> *'Twas truth's gray dawn across the night;*
> *Yet on this world we trust will shine*
> *Some larger beams of light divine.*
> *As one by one the shadows flee,*
> *We seek the faith that is to be.*
>
> *A faith where truth shall not be feared,*
> *But to it temples shall be reared;*
> *Where beauty unashamed shall dwell*
> *With goodness, and its secrets tell;*
> *Where love shall reign supreme, and we*
> *Shall live the faith that is to be.*

CPSIA information can be obtained
at www.ICGtesting.com
Printed in the USA
FFOW02n0631150414
4816FF